THE
GOSPEL
OF GOD

WATCHMAN NEE

Living Stream Ministry
Anaheim, California

First Edition, July 1990.

ISBN 1-57593-953-3

Published by

Living Stream Ministry
1853 W. Ball Road, Anaheim, CA 92804 U.S.A.
P. O. Box 2121, Anaheim, CA 92814 U.S.A.

Printed in the United States of America

97 98 99 00 01 02 / 10 9 8 7 6 5 4 3

CONTENTS

PREFACE TO THE ENGLISH EDITION

As has become manifest to Christian readers throughout the earth, Brother Watchman Nee was especially entrusted by the Lord with the burden to help the believers in the truth of God's full salvation. In the spring of 1937 Watchman Nee delivered a series of twenty-six messages on the basic truths of the gospel of God to the church in Shanghai, China. These messages compose the contents of this two-volume set. The matters covered are comprehensive, ranging from man's sinful condition before salvation to his destiny in the coming age. In the first volume, Watchman Nee presents the particulars of God's salvation, that is, man's sins; God's love, grace, and mercy; the nature of grace; the function of the law and God's righteousness; the work of Christ and of the Holy Spirit in God's salvation; and faith as the way of salvation. In the second volume, he covers in detail the issues of eternal security of salvation and God's way of dealing with the believer's sins both in this age and in the age to come. For both issues Watchman Nee presents persuasive reponses from the Scriptures to various understandings current among Christians.

The messages in this series were spoken by Watchman Nee in Chinese and were transcribed by hand as they were being given. The handwritten notes have been translated into English and edited as necessary. As much as possible, the spoken nature of the messages has been preserved. Many of the illustrations Brother Nee used were drawn from his life in China at the time.

These messages demonstrate the Lord's commission to our brother and His equipping of him with the revelation in His Word. May the Lord richly bless all who read and see these truths released by the Lord through our brother.

The Editor

CHAPTER FIFTEEN

SALVATION BEING ETERNAL— POSITIVE REASONS

(1)

In the last few messages, we saw that there is a distinction between sin and sins in man. We saw how God loves us and gives His grace to us, how His grace is manifested in His righteousness, how the Lord Jesus has accomplished all the work for us, and what His death and resurrection have done. Furthermore, we saw how man can receive God's salvation. Man does not receive God's salvation through the law, good works, confession, prayer, and many other things. In the last message, we saw how to believe and what faith is. In this message, we will continue with our study.

The Bible shows us that the duration of God's salvation is eternal; it is not temporal. In other words, God's salvation is given to man eternally, rather than temporarily. Once a Christian is saved, there is no possibility for him to perish. I am not saying that there is no chastisement for a Christian once he is saved. Neither am I saying that there will not be judgment and loss of reward if a Christian is not faithful in the Lord's work after his salvation. A Christian can be disciplined in this age, and also be punished in the millennium. I am not saying that a sinner will be disciplined. I am saying that a believer whose work is not approved by the Lord will lose his reward at the time of the judgment seat of Christ. If a believer has sins that have not been repented of in this age, he will receive definite punishment in the coming kingdom. All of these are truths in the Bible.

The Bible also shows us that there is no possibility of a

Christian being lost again, once he is saved. In other words, once we have been saved before God, we are eternally saved. Man always has the thought that even though he is saved, he does not know whether he will become unsaved after a while. God says that we have passed out of death into life (John 5:24). But we wonder whether or not we can pass out of life into death. God says that we will not perish but will have eternal life (3:16). But we wonder if we will not have eternal life but will perish. We do not know if our salvation before God can be shaken. However, after we read the Word of God carefully, we find that once a person is saved, he is eternally saved. We want to consider this question from two sides. First, we want to consider it from the positive side. Later, we will consider it from the negative side.

In this message, we want to see from the Bible how God's salvation is eternal. If God's salvation could be lost, what would happen to man? Later, we will consider this matter from the negative side. We will consider verse by verse all the Scripture that seemingly speaks of salvation not being eternal and being able to be lost. We will see whether or not the salvation granted to us by God can be lost. In this message we will consider what is mentioned on the positive side. We must see clearly whether or not the Bible says that we can lose the salvation that we have received.

GOD'S GRACE AND LOVE

We have previously mentioned what grace is. All of the readers of the New Testament know that we are saved by grace. No one would be so incorrect as to say that salvation is by the law and not by grace. If a man says that a person is saved by the law and not by grace, he has never read the New Testament. This light is too great in the New Testament. Some things we can let go of easily. But we cannot let this matter go by in a light way. If salvation is by grace, then we can never be a debtor before God. If I show grace to others, I cannot expect any repayment. If I had any thought of repayment, and if I had any hope of being repaid, this would be a loan and not grace. If I give something to you with the hope that one day you will return it, this is not grace. If God gives us grace today with the hope that we will render good works to Him later, it is not grace either. There is absolutely no return regarding grace.

What does the Bible say about the way to receive eternal life? The gift of God is eternal life in Christ (Rom. 6:23). Therefore, the eternal life that we have received cannot be lost. What is a gift? A gift is a present from God. It is something that God gives to us. If others give something to us, can they ask for it back? We are not kindergarten children, giving others some candy one day and asking for it in return the next day. A gift is something given freely. If our salvation could be lost, Romans 6:23 would have to say, "The loan of God is eternal life in Christ." A loan can be reclaimed, but something that is given cannot be reclaimed. Once it is given, it is given forever. If eternal life is given to us in Christ, then it can never be reclaimed. The word *gift* in the original language clearly indicates that it is something given freely; it cannot be reclaimed. If it cannot be reclaimed, then there is no possibility of us losing the gift.

The Bible shows us clearly that God's gift is without repentance. Eternal life is an important item of God's gift. Salvation is also an important item of God's gift. There are many other items besides these. God's gift is given without repentance. If there is no repentance, how can God reclaim it? In order to reclaim it, there must first be regret. Without any regret, there can never be any reclaiming. At the same time, if there is any reclaiming, it is no longer a gift. With giving, there is no such thing as reclaiming. Can I say that I am giving something and then claim it back again tomorrow? I cannot do that. If it is given, it cannot be reclaimed.

God is not like us, wavering and changing frequently. He is not one way today and another way the next. Once God has given us something, He will never claim it back. As far as God's character is concerned, salvation is given to us as a gift rather than as a loan. Hence, we have to admit that it is eternal. Thank and praise the Lord that God never borrows and never lends. He never expects repayment; He only gives. God is too great. Not only does He never borrow or lend, He never sells either. God saves us by grace. God is so great that He cannot sell, borrow, or lend anything. He is so great that He can only give away. Hence, we see that the gift of God is eternal life.

Why does God have to give us eternal life? Why does He have to give us the gift in His Son? Most have probably read John 3:16 which says, "For God so loved the world that He gave His only begotten Son, that every one who believes into Him would not perish, but would have eternal life." Why did God give His Son to the world? It is because He loves us. Why did God give to us eternal life? It is also because He loves us. If while we were yet sinners, God loved us to such an extent that He gave us the life of His Son, is it possible that after we become Christians and are weak and short of God's glory that He would reject us? If God's Son can die for us on the cross while we were yet sinners, can He refuse to love us after we have believed in Him merely because we are a little weak? If God's love cannot change, then there is no possibility for His grace to change either. He was so willing to give up His only begotten Son to die for our sins, and He had such a great love for us. Since the time He showed such love to us, has He completely changed? Does it mean that now that we have become Christians, He has decided to cast us into hell and not love us anymore? Humanly speaking, if He previously loved us so much that He would die on the cross for us, how could He have such a change today? How could we be unsaved again? This is impossible.

Not only is this impossible according to human reason, but God's Word also says the same thing. John 13:1 says, "Jesus...having loved His own who were in the world, He loved them to the uttermost." Hence, there is no change in the love with which God loves men. Inasmuch as His heart was full of love for us when He went to the cross, God is still loving us today. His love has not changed. His grace has not changed either. If we think that there is the possibility for salvation and eternal life to be lost, then we have to conclude that there is the possibility for God's love to change. But this is impossible! If the source cannot change, then the outflow will never change. If the life does not change, then the fruit produced cannot change. We must know God's heart. We must realize that God cannot claim His Son back. Romans 8:32 indicates that since God is willing to give us His Son, He cannot claim Him back.

Which do you think is greater: the Son of God or our salvation? Is the Son of God more precious? Or is the life that we have received more precious? Because we are fleshly, we think that the Savior is not that important, and that life is more important than the Savior. As long as we have life, everything is all right. We are not that concerned about the Savior. But in God's eyes, the Savior is more precious. He is more precious than our life. The Son of God is more precious than the life that we received. Hence, Romans 8:32 tells us that if God did not spare His own Son, but delivered Him up for us all, how shall He not also with Him freely give us all things? If God is willing to give up His Son for our sins, and if He is willing to give us this very Son freely, would He consider taking eternal life back from us after some consideration? Suppose a brother owes me ten thousand dollars and cannot repay this amount. If I am a rich man, I may say to him, "You are not able to pay your debt. But I am gracious. Here is ten thousand dollars. Take it so that you can pay your debt." Later, we may ride a tramway to the pier. The tram fare costs eight cents per person, but he may only have seven cents. He may say to me, "Can you give me one penny, for I am short one cent." I not only have many more pennies, but bank notes and other cash as well. But what if I asked him for the money back and told him that he had to pay back the penny. Would you not feel strange if I did this? Yesterday I gave him ten thousand dollars. Today I do not let him go for one penny. What is this? You would probably say that I have a high fever and that I am sick. Why would I not care about ten thousand dollars yet be concerned for one penny? If God has given us His only begotten Son through His great love, would He argue with us about the salvation that we have received? We must remember that the difference between one penny and ten thousand dollars is far less than the difference between life and the Savior, between life and the Lord of life, and between the salvation we received and the only begotten Son of God. Since God has given us His only begotten Son, how can He ask for salvation back? For man to have such a thought shows not only ignorance and a lack of understanding concerning God's grace and love, but sheer unsoundness of mind. Only those who are unclear and unsound in their mind would say such a thing.

Thank God that He has given us His Son; He will not claim Him back. Besides His Son, He has also given us many other things such as eternal life and salvation. God has given us His Son and has also given us eternal life. If He cannot reclaim His Son, then neither can He reclaim the eternal life that we have received. Hence, according to God's grace, it is impossible to lose the salvation and the life that we have received. This is God's clear word to us.

GOD SAVING US WITH A PLAN

Second, is our salvation an accident or a purposeful act of God? Is God's salvation like giving two pennies to a beggar that one happens to come across in the street? Or is God purposefully seeking to find a man to whom He can give money? Is God's salvation an accident, or is it according to a definite plan? Those who do not understand salvation may think that God's salvation is an accident. But all those who understand the Bible and who know God realize that His salvation is not an accident. Instead, it was planned long ago according to a definite plan. Romans 8:29 says, "Those whom He foreknew, He also predestinated to be conformed to the image of His Son." Verse 30, a parenthetical word, says, "And those whom He predestinated, these He also called; and those whom He called, these He also justified; and those whom He justified, these He also glorified." The salvation that we are talking about involves all the things covered in verses 29 and 30. The history of our salvation began with justification in verse 30. We were saved at the time that we were justified. We only know that we have believed in Jesus and that we have been saved and justified. We think that justification is our first encounter with God. We think that the first time we touched God in our life was when we were justified. But the Bible says that God touched us long ago. He knew us long ago. Our justification came afterwards. God's knowledge of us came first.

Some have said that Romans 8:29-30 is the only chain in the entire Bible. It is a chain of different rings linked together. This is a most precious and complete chain. The first ring of this chain is God's foreknowledge of man. The second ring is our predestination to be conformed to the image of His Son. The third ring is the calling of those who have been predestinated. The fourth ring is the justification of those who have been called. The fifth ring is the glorification of those who have been justified. It is a series of rings linked to one another. We think that we first knew God when we were saved and justified. But the Bible says that before we were saved and justified, God knew us already. Those whom God knew long ago, He marked out. To be marked out means to have a check mark put by our name, indicating that He has claimed us for Himself. For what purpose were we marked out? It is so that we would be like His unique Son, Jesus Christ. He not only wants one Son, Jesus Christ; He came to mark us out so that we would be identical to His Son. Those who were marked out are called. The ones who are called are known by Him. He called the ones whom He knew and marked out. After He called them, He justified them.

If justification is the first step in a Christian's relationship with God, it does not matter much for us not to be justified again in the future. If I pick up two pennies today and throw them into the fire tomorrow, it does not matter much to me. Not to be justified is, of course, a loss on man's part. But God suffers no loss. However, we have to know that the history of our relationship with God does not start from justification and salvation. Rather, it starts from God's foreknowledge. God's foreknowledge is the beginning of everything. To be marked out is the second step. To be called is the third step. Only after the third step do we have justification. If we were to lose our justification and become sinners again, we would put a question mark on God's omniscience. Since God foreknew us and marked us out, how can we still perish after we are saved? A person predestinated by God can never be thrown into hell and burned like a piece of wood.

It is a simple thing for us to make a decision because we change so easily. One minute we can be in heaven, and the next minute we can be in hell. We may change once a day for the three hundred and sixty-five days of the year. But since God is God, His foreknowledge and predestination cannot be shaken. The God whom we know and whom we worship cannot change what He has decided. Because He has the foreknowledge, the predestination, and the calling, our justification is eternal. It is a small thing for us to lose our justification. But it is a great thing for God to lose His foreknowledge. For us to lose our justification does not mean much. But for God to make a mistake in foreknowing and calling us is a serious thing. God cannot annul justification without affecting His foreknowledge, predestination, and calling. If you take away one ring, the other three rings will not stand. Whenever our salvation is lost, God's foreknowledge, predestination, and calling are all negated.

In addition, there is another item. The Lord says, "Those whom He justified, these He also glorified" (v. 30). Unless God brings those whom He justified into glory, His work is not complete. If we cannot get into the new heaven and the new earth, and if we cannot enter into eternal glory, God's work is not complete. The last ring of God's work is glory. Until we are in glory, God's work is not complete. This is God's Word. What are we going to do with it? We cannot set it aside. God says that those whom He justified will enter into glory unconditionally. He does not say that those who are justified will enter into glory if they have good works. He does not say that only those whose works are approved can enter into glory. Neither does God say that those whom He justified must also be considered saved by man before they can enter into glory. There are no such conditions. All of the things that are mentioned here are related to God. It is God who foreknew. It is God who predestinated. It is God who destined us to be like His Son and to be conformed to the image of the Son of God. It is God who has called us and justified us. It is God who will bring us, the justified ones, into glory. It is also God who will bring us into the new heaven and the new earth to inherit the eternal glory.

Which of the rings is the greatest in the Bible? Some say that glory is the greatest. Others say that foreknowledge is the greatest. Actually, there is no difference between them; every one is the same. We cannot say one is greater than the others. As many as God foreknew, that many are marked out. As many as are marked out, that many are called. As many as are called, that many are justified. As many as are justified, that many will enter into glory. Hallelujah! Can God foreknow that one hundred will be saved, but mark out only ninety, call only eighty, justify fifty, and merely bring ten into glory? God cannot change. It is impossible to mark out many and call a few. Please remember that the words "those whom" in these verses convey this meaning. "Those whom" He foreknew, these He also predestinated. "Those whom" He predestinated, these He also called. "Those whom" He called, these He also justified. "Those whom" He justified, these He also glorified. These "those whoms" join the five rings together. In the original language, the word "these" means "these people." So, those whom He foreknew, "these people" He also marked out. Those whom He marked out, "these people" He also called. Those whom He called, "these people" He also justified. Those whom He justified, "these people" He also glorified. We cannot be short of any one item. These are all works of God. If they were our works, we could get some saved by mistake because we do not know which ones should be saved. But if they are God's works, there can be no mistake. If we do not know God and His works, we may still think that there is the possibility of losing some people. But if we know God and His works, we will realize that no one can be subtracted or added.

The Bible says that God is eternal; He is not like us, having a beginning without an ending. God says that He is the beginning and the end, the Alpha and the Omega (Rev. 22:13). He says that He is the beginning and the ending. We sometimes have a beginning without an ending. At other times we have a good ending, but we do not know how to have a good beginning. But God is both the beginning and the end. God's work cannot stop halfway. If salvation is only the result of our work, then failing in regard to the matter of salvation

only means that we have stopped halfway. But we know that
salvation is God's work. It is God who has saved us. Hence,
if we cannot be saved to the uttermost, this does not mean
that we have stopped halfway; it means that God has stopped
halfway. Certainly, we can never imagine that God can stop
halfway.

Philippians 1:6 says that God has begun a good work in
us. Since God has started it and has given us salvation
Himself, He must complete this work until the day of Christ
Jesus. We must remember that the work of God never stops
halfway. He will complete this work until the day of Christ
Jesus, that is, until God glorifies us. We can see how
far-reaching is God's Word, how wide its scope, how long it
lasts, and how deep its roots. Verse 6 says, "Being confident
of this very thing, that He who has begun in you a good work
will complete it until the day of Christ Jesus." Either God
will not start, or He will have to finish what He has started.
If God was not willing to save us, that would be the end of
the story. But if God's desire is to save us, there will be no
way for us not to be saved. Therefore, we can say, "God, we
thank and praise You, because our salvation is eternally
secure." If it were up to us to follow up, we would fail. The
work of following up is accomplished by Him; the work of
preservation is also accomplished by Him. We can never follow
up what He has started.

When I was in school, I had to practice Chinese calligraphy. Many times I was too lazy to do it, so I asked some
classmates who were good at it to do it for me. Of course,
later I made confession of this sin. Every week we had to
submit five pages of calligraphy. All of them were done by
my classmates. On one occasion after my classmate had
finished one line of calligraphy, he was called away. He told
me that he was busy and that I should finish what he had
started. When I picked up the brush, I realized that I could
never follow up on what he had started. His calligraphy was
so fine that my characters simply could not match his. In the
same way, the work of salvation was started by God. He must
be the One to conclude it. If we had to conclude it, we would
never make it. If the work of salvation began with God and

was followed up by us, none of us would be qualified to be saved. All those who want to follow up do not know God and do not know themselves. If we know Him, we will realize that there is no way for us to finish whatever He has begun. And if we really know ourselves, we will realize that we simply cannot follow up. The entire work of salvation is accomplished by Him. He has given us salvation. He will save us to the uttermost. We do nothing to preserve our salvation.

Hence, we see two things here. First, because the nature of God's salvation is grace, it is impossible for us to lose it. Second, since it is God who has started the work, who has foreknown and predestinated us, who has called and justified us, who has saved us, and who will bring us into glory, God's attribute would be put into question if we lost our salvation.

REGENERATION AND ETERNAL LIFE

The third point that we need to consider is the salvation that God has given us. What has God done for us, and what has He given us? We all know that God has given us His life. He has regenerated us. All those who believe in Him and who receive Him are given the authority to become children of God (John 1:12). We are begotten of God, and we have the authority to become His children (vv. 12-13). John 3 says that we are to be born anew; it is the Holy Spirit who has regenerated us (v. 6). The first Epistle of John tells us how man can be regenerated. First John 5:1 says that everyone who believes that Jesus is the Christ has been begotten of God. How are we regenerated? We are regenerated through believing in Jesus as the Christ whom God appointed. After reading the above three verses, we can realize who we, as Christians, are. We are the children of God. When a sinner believes in the Lord Jesus and is saved, God gives him a new life. This is regeneration. The Bible shows us in at least three or four places that being regenerated is to receive eternal life. The Bible repeatedly shows us that those who receive eternal life are the ones who have believed, and those who believe have eternal life. This is shown to us repeatedly by the Gospel of John.

Here we have a problem. God has given to us eternal life,

but what should we do? We must realize that this is both
the beginning and the end. If I do not desire to have a
relationship with someone, I have to approach it in one of
two ways. Since human relationships are bilateral, they
always have two sides. Therefore, not having a relationship
also involves two sides. First, there must not be a beginning.
If there is not a beginning, there will not even be a relationship. Second, the relationship can terminate and die, in
which case there will no longer be a relationship. For
example, suppose I am a very bad son, a prodigal. There are
two ways for my father not to have a relationship with me.
First, he should not have begotten me. If there had not been
a beginning, he would not have to be related to me. But if
there has been a beginning, he cannot use the first way anymore. In this case, he can only wait day by day for me to
die. When I die, my relationship with him will be over. If I
am not born of him, I will have nothing to do with him. If
I have died, I will also have nothing to do with him anymore.

What happened between God and us? God has begotten
us. At the time that we believed in Jesus, God begat us with
His Spirit and with His own life. We have become the children
of God. Can this relationship be severed? If you have a son
today who is bad, undisciplined, and lawless, you can disown
him in court. But the fact that you have begotten him still
remains. He is still your son in reality. Today God has
begotten us. Can He say that He has not begotten us? Even
if we become worse than we are, we are still begotten of
Him. Even if our father denies us, we are still begotten
of him. No one can deny the fact of begetting. A good son is
begotten of his father. A bad son is also begotten of his father.
No one can nullify this relationship. Hence, when God
justified us, He did not do it in the way that a person sends
people away on the street with two pennies. He said that He
has begotten us. God is in Spirit, and we are also in spirit.
God and we have a father-son relationship. This is what God
Himself has said. He has given us authority to become
children of God. He has given to us eternal life. We are
children of God by authority. That is the beginning.

What then can God do now? He can only hope for us to

die. But the strange thing is that our relationship with Him begins with regeneration and ends with eternal life. Not only has God begotten us, He has also given us eternal life. If God had started the work but had been unable to complete it, we would be finished. In that case, we could not be saved. As far as the eternal life that we received from God is concerned, it is impossible for God not to save us. Thank the Lord that He has regenerated us and has given us eternal life, which is the life of His Son. If there is a man today who thinks that a Christian can perish again if he becomes weak and that only a good son will have eternal life, while a bad son will perish, this man does not know God's salvation. He may think that the Lord is a debt collector, coming to collect eternal life and redemption. If we do well, we can keep them. If we do not do well, He will take them back. This is not the salvation of God. The beginning has to be of Him. The continuation also has to be of Him. Since God has given us salvation, how can we lose our salvation? Since God has started this relationship, and the life we received is an eternal life which can never cease to exist, we can never perish again.

God gave us another type in the Bible to show us that we can never lose our salvation once we have received it from God. Genesis 3 is a familiar passage to us. It tells us how Adam sinned. After Adam ate of the fruit of the tree of knowledge of good and evil, God drove him from the garden of Eden and guarded the way to the tree of life with the cherubim and the flaming sword that turned every way (v. 24). Why did God have to surround the entrance to the tree of life with the flaming sword and the cherubim? Why did He not allow Adam to eat of the fruit of the tree of life? Genesis 3:22 says, "And the Lord God said, Behold, the man is become as one of us, to know good and evil: and now, lest he put forth his hand, and take also of the tree of life, and eat, and live for ever." Here we see a picture. We all know that the fruit of the tree of knowledge of good and evil signifies independence from God. The fruit of the tree of life, on the other hand, signifies life—the life given to us by the Son of God. After Adam sinned, God was afraid that Adam would eat of the fruit of the tree of life and that if he ate

of it, he would not die. If Adam could still die after eating
the fruit of the tree of life, then why did God have to do so
much work? Why did He have to guard the way to the tree
of life with the cherubim and the flaming sword? God did
this because He was afraid that Adam would live forever if
he ate of it.

We are those who have been redeemed. What we have
eaten is not the fruit of the tree of life, which is a type only.
We have eaten Life Himself. Can we still die? If Adam could
not die after having eaten a symbolic fruit, how can we die
after having been washed by the blood of the Lord Jesus,
having eaten of the tree of life itself, and having received
eternal life? Adam knew the tree of life as a type, whereas
we have received what the tree of life typifies. How can we
possibly die? Only those who do not know what regeneration
is and what eternal life is can say that salvation can be lost.
Thank the Lord that eternal life is a fact that can never be
annulled. It is a history that can never be blotted out. This
is why we can live before God. What grace God has bestowed
upon us! The relationship between God and us is such that
we can strongly say that no power on earth can separate us
from Him. Even if God were to be unhappy about it, He
cannot annul this relationship.

WE BEING THE MEMBERS OF CHRIST

Let us look at a fourth point. When we were saved, not
only did God regenerate us and give us eternal life; He made
us one spirit with the Lord. First Corinthians tells us that
we have not only become one spirit with Christ, but we have
become members of His Body (12:27). In 1 Corinthians 6:15
we have the same word. It says that our bodies are the
members of Christ. Hence, when an unbeliever is saved, not
only has he received regeneration and eternal life from God,
but he at the same time is joined to the Body of Christ to
become a member of the Body of Christ. The Bible says that
we are the Body of Christ.

If God saves us one by one in Christ, and if Christ died
for us, washed away our sins, gave us eternal life, and caused
us to have a life relationship with Him to become His

members, what is our end? Salvation includes being a member of the Body of Christ. If we were to perish, what would the end be? The end would be that the Body of Christ would be maimed. This Body would either be short of an ear or short of half a nose. It would either be one finger short or one toe short. The Body of Christ is a definite truth in the Bible. It is a concrete thing. If we have become one Body with Christ after being saved, the perishing of any one person will mean the missing of a part of the Body of Christ, and the Body of Christ will be maimed.

Once a black slave woman was working in the home of a white family. The lady of the house was a nominal Christian, but the black woman was a genuine believer. All day long the slave woman sang joyously. The lady was so bothered by the joyous singing that she could not refrain from asking why she was so happy. The woman told her, "Don't you know that God has sent His Son, Jesus Christ, to wash away all of our sins? Don't you know that we will be with God in the future? Why should I not be joyous?" The lady asked, "How do you know that you will be with God in the future? What happens if you are lost?" The slave said, "The Lord Jesus told us that the Father is greater than all. I am in my Father's hands. These hands are upholding me and preserving me. How can I be lost?" The lady thought about it for a while and then said, "But you are a fool! If God is greater than all, His hands would be large! If things can slip through your fingers, then things can slip through His fingers also. Since His hands are large, the space between His fingers must also be wide. If you slip through His fingers, He would not even notice it. You claim that His hands will protect you. But God is so great, and you are so small. There is no comparison between you and God. If you slip out of His hand, He will not know it." The woman answered, "Madam, you do not understand. I am not only in His hand, I am a little finger in His hand. If I were only in His hand, He may not notice when I slip out. But if I am a little finger in God's hand, how can I slip away?" If a man has believed and has become a Christian, he is a member of the Body of Christ and is a little finger in God's hand. If I am a member of the Body of Christ, God

will never allow me, as a member, to slip away. I thank the
Lord today that I can never slip away.

First Corinthians 12 says that if one member in the body
suffers, all the members suffer (v. 26). We cannot have one
finger hurting while the other members remain unaffected.
If every believer is a member in the Body of Christ, then if
one day one of us were to suffer in hell, everyone else would
feel the hurt in heaven. If one person perishes, then every
Christian will have to perish as well. This is the oneness of
the Body of Christ.

Not only does 1 Corinthians tell us that we are the
members of the Body of Christ, but other books tell us the
same. The book of Ephesians talks about the process that
the Body of Christ goes through. It also says that we are the
members of Christ, but in a different way. First Corinthians
talks about the relationship and sphere of the members.
Ephesians talks about the future of the members. Ephesians
5:29-30 says clearly, "For no one ever hated his own flesh,
but nourishes and cherishes it, even as Christ also the church,
because we are members of His Body." We are the members
of the Body of Christ. Let us read the preceding verses.
Verses 25 through 27 say, "Husbands, love your wives even
as Christ also loved the church and gave Himself up for her
that He might sanctify her, cleansing her by the washing of
the water in the word, that He might present the church to
Himself glorious, not having spot or wrinkle or any such
things, but that she would be holy and without blemish." If
we read the entire portion from verse 25 to verse 30, we will
discover one thing—the church is the Body of Christ. Christ
is washing the church by the water in the word. He will
continually wash her until she becomes holy. The end is to
present her to Himself a glorious church. If there are any
lost ones in the church, we will have a maimed Body, and
there will not be the presenting of a glorious church. The
persons will not even remain, much less the glorious church.
This church has no spot or wrinkle or any such things. What
does this mean? Ephesians 5 explains, "But that she would
be holy and without blemish." To be without blemish is to be
without any spot. If it is possible for the members of Christ

to perish, then not only will there be blemishes, but maimed parts as well. But the Bible says that this Body is not only without maimed members; it is without any blemish.

Hence, we cannot lose our salvation. Since Christ will have a glorious church without spot or wrinkle, one that will be presented to Him holy and without blemish, none of us can perish.

WE BEING THE SPIRITUAL HOUSE GOD IS BUILDING

Fifth, the church is not only a Body. When the individual Christians come together before God, they become a temple. Every Christian is like a stone, and the church is the spiritual house that God is building. The Lord Jesus is the foundation of this spiritual temple. He is a great stone. Every Christian is a small stone built upon the Lord Jesus to become the temple of God and the habitation of God. This is what is spoken of in 1 Peter 2:5. If there were a possibility for Christians to perish, the temple of God would become more unsightly than our run-down meeting hall; one minute the stones would be taken out, and another minute they would be put back in again, and the walls would be full of holes. If that were the case, why would God not make up His mind before He saved men? God intends that we be built up into a spiritual house. If it is a spiritual house, then not one stone can be lost. If any stone can be lost, the spiritual house would be in trouble and would not be up to standard.

The Old Testament record in 1 Kings 6:7 tells us how the temple of Solomon was built. Chapter five is an account of Solomon sending men to the mountains to cut the stones. The stones were cut in the mountains. By chapter six, they were moved to mount Moriah for the building. Hence, when the temple was being built, there was no sound from iron tools. There was no need for further cutting. The skilled workmen had calculated accurately and prepared everything on the mountain before the materials were moved to the building. There was no more need of improvement; everything was done properly. If while building the earthly temple, Solomon's skilled men could cut the stones so well that they were exact in every way and had no need for improvement, could God change us, the living stones, once every two or three days when He builds the spiritual temple? Could God have such oversight? Would God not know how to calculate? Is God worse than man? In the Old Testament, God used men to build. In the New Testament, He builds by Himself. Is God's own work inferior to man's? If the believers are stones for the building of the spiritual house, can they be lost? Therefore, if we are in God's temple, we can never be lost.

HAVING THE HOLY SPIRIT
AS THE SEAL AND THE PLEDGE

Sixth, there is another very important and wonderful thing. At the time that every unbeliever is saved, not only does he receive eternal life and become a member of the Body of Christ and a living stone in the temple, but he receives the Holy Spirit as a seal. God places the Holy Spirit in him as a seal. Ephesians 1:13 says, "In whom you also, having heard the word of the truth, the gospel of your salvation, in Him also believing, you were sealed with the Holy Spirit of the promise." Is that not our history? We have heard the gospel of our salvation and have believed in Christ. What happened after we believed? We were sealed with the Holy Spirit of the promise. Every Christian has the Holy Spirit as the seal. It is very obvious that the Holy Spirit does not belong just to some special Christians and that only specially sanctified Christians have life. Verse 13 says that all who have heard the gospel of salvation and who have believed, have received the Holy Spirit as the seal. This proves that the seal of the Holy Spirit is something that all Christians have in common. As soon as one believes, he is saved and has the Holy Spirit as the seal.

What does it mean for a Christian to have the Holy Spirit as the seal? What is a seal? There are over three million people in Shanghai. How does God know who belongs to Him and who does not? If you bring me a Bible today, how do I know that it is yours? There are countless Bibles like yours. The Bible Society recently published a report saying that it sold over eleven million Bibles last year. Among all those Bibles, how do you know which one is yours? When you go home and put a seal on your Bible you know that it is yours. Even if you were to mix this Bible with all the Bibles in the world, you could still identify it as yours. Today, because there are so many people in the world, how do you know who belongs to God and who does not? God has put a seal on you, proving that you belong to Him. God did not seal you on your forehead with a large wooden chop. He is not like the coming Antichrist, who will place a mark on man's forehead. God put the Holy Spirit in you as a seal. All those who have the Holy Spirit belong to God. All those who do not have the Holy Spirit do not belong to God. At the time a person is saved, God does a sealing work on him and puts the Holy Spirit within him to prove that he is of God.

If the seal of the Holy Spirit in us can be erased, then it is possible for us to perish; we may be considered as not belonging to Him. We may be considered as typical people in the world or even as God's enemy. But if this seal is within us, then we belong to God. How long will the seal of God be in us? The last part of Ephesians 4:30 says, "In whom you were sealed unto the day of redemption." "Whom" refers to the Holy Spirit. The previous clause says, "And do not grieve the Holy Spirit of God." This seal will last unto the day of redemption. How long does the Bible say that we will have the seal of the Holy Spirit? We will not have it for merely three or five years, or for three or five hundred years, but until the day of redemption. What is the day of redemption? Romans 8 says that the day of redemption is the day when the Lord Jesus will come back. The day of redemption is the day when our bodies will be redeemed (v. 23). Hence, this denotes the day when the Lord Jesus comes back. The seal of the Holy Spirit remains in us until the coming again of the Lord Jesus.

When the Lord Jesus comes again (not the time of the first rapture at the beginning of the tribulation, but at the time that the whole Body will be raptured), all the believers will be taken up into the air. The Lord Jesus will send the angels to come and gather these believers. The angels are limited. They are not omniscient; they do not know everything. The angels are the servants sent out to invite the

guests. When these angels see all those with the seal of the
Holy Spirit, they will gather them. Hence, the Holy Spirit is
not in us for three or five days, or for three or five hundred
days, but in us until the day of rapture. Today if a man says
that he can lose his salvation and perish, then I will ask him
what he will do with the seal of the Holy Spirit. Since God
has said that we have been sealed by Him, there is nothing
we can do to remove this seal. God has said that this seal
will remain until the day of Jesus Christ and the day of
rapture.

In John 14 the Lord Jesus said that the Holy Spirit will
be with us forever (v. 16). Once the Holy Spirit of the New
Testament comes into us, He will never leave us. Never believe
in the diagram that some Christians display, which depicts
a man with a heart full of snakes, pigs, dogs, and many other
animals. Next to the heart is a dove representing the Holy
Spirit. When a person's heart is clean, the Holy Spirit
supposedly will come into him and stay there, and all the
other animals will depart. But if his heart is not clean, the
dove will fly away, and all the other things will come in. This
is absolutely wrong! The Holy Spirit can never fly away.

The Bible says that we should not grieve the Holy Spirit
(Eph. 4:30). Grief is the expression of love; anger is the
expression of hate. Wherever there is hate, there is anger.
Wherever there is love, there is grief. Please remember that
both anger and grief come from mistakes. In both cases they
are caused by mistakes. If there is love, mistakes will result
in grief. If there is hate, mistakes will result in anger. If you
love a person, you will grieve for his mistakes. If you hate a
person, you will be angry about his mistakes. Both are caused
by the same thing—mistakes. But the results are different.
Here, it is not anger, but grief. The Word does not say not
to anger the Holy Spirit. Rather, it says not to grieve the
Holy Spirit. He is not upon us, but in us. When He sees our
failure, He grieves within us; He will not go away. Why will
He not go away? It is because He is a seal. As a seal, He
will be in us until the day of redemption. If we read the
Word of God, we will not be able to deny this fact.

In the Old Testament, Psalm 51 records a very precious

prayer. There David prayed that the Lord would not take His Spirit of holiness from him (v. 11). But in the New Testament, no believer can pray this prayer. Those who do not know the Bible may pray that God would not take the Holy Spirit from them. But those who know the Word of God know that the Holy Spirit can only be grieved within us; He will not go away. I am not saying that it is all right for Christians to sin. I am saying that at the time that we were saved, the Holy Spirit entered into us to be our seal. This fact has nothing to do with our weakness or our sin. The two are entirely different matters.

If we perish, who really suffers? If I lose a hymn book, of course, the hymn book suffers. But the first one to suffer is me. I have spent the effort to obtain the hymn book. I have paid the price and the money to obtain it. Hence, I am the one who suffers the most. How did God gain us? We were dead in sin and fallen. God caused His Son to die for us and shed His blood to redeem us with a great price. Do not think that if we lose our salvation only we have lost it and only we have suffered. Remember that we have been purchased by God. If we lose our salvation, God will also lose something. We have been purchased by His blood. Why does God preserve us? God preserves us for His own sake. If we are lost, the One who suffers is not us, but God.

The biggest problem today is that we do not believe how important we are in God's hands. Man finds it difficult to believe that God loves him. He finds it difficult to believe that God wants him. He always thinks that he is dispensable to God. God has given up His Son for our sake and has sent His Son into the world to pass through all the sufferings for our sake. He was crucified on the cross for the purpose of gaining us. If He does not care, then who would care? If I do not safeguard my hymn book, would my hymn book keep track of itself? Ephesians 1:13 says that the Holy Spirit is in us as a seal. Following this, verse 14 tells us that the Holy Spirit comes to be the seal because we are God's acquired possession. Therefore, we can tell the entire world that we are God's possession. It is not a question of our losing or not losing. It is a question of God's losing or not losing. It is not we who are keeping watch. We do not have to exhaust our mind over this matter. The whole work is His. If it were not, why would He send His only begotten Son to the cross? If He has exerted great effort and paid a great price to send His Son to the cross, He must exert greater effort and pay a greater price to keep us from being lost.

Suppose we have a most precious and expensive diamond ring, a very precious pearl, or an expensive gem. However much we spent to acquire it, we will spend the same amount to preserve it. If we bought it for ten thousand dollars, we would not lose it easily; we would surely guard it closely. We have to realize that we have been purchased by God with the greatest price. We were saved by the Son of God. The Son of God is greater than the entire world and the entire universe. Do not think that God does not care for us. God treats us in the same way that we treat our own treasure. It was the good shepherd that sought out the sheep (Luke 15). It was not the sheep that sought out the good shepherd. The Lord Jesus said that one day He would die for even one of His lost ones. It is not the sheep's business. It is the good shepherd who died for the sheep. Before God, we are those who have been purchased by Him. If we are lost, God is the One who will suffer. Therefore, we must remember that since we have the Holy Spirit as a seal, there is no possibility for us to be lost.

Can the grace which God gives to man be preserved by man? If it were preserved by man, we would have lost it long ago. Not only would we have lost it, even Peter and Paul would have lost it. We have to realize that God has already set us aside completely. Everything is of God. God alone has saved us. God alone is preserving us. May God show us clearly how long our salvation lasts, so that we can remove all fleshly thoughts and accept His thoughts.

CHAPTER SIXTEEN

SALVATION BEING ETERNAL—
POSITIVE REASONS

(2)

Last evening we saw a number of things that God has already done. When we were saved, God gave us His Holy Spirit as the seal. It is not that the Holy Spirit seals a seal upon us, but that the Holy Spirit is a seal upon us; the Holy Spirit is the seal of God upon us. This seal will remain until the day of redemption. Therefore, not one Christian can lose his salvation. Tonight we shall continue to see that the Holy Spirit is not merely the seal given to us by God, but also the pledge given to us by God to assure us of our eternal inheritance. The Holy Spirit is the proof of our receiving the inheritance.

Here we see that there are two aspects to the Holy Spirit in us. On the one hand, God puts His Holy Spirit in us as the seal to prove that we belong to God; on the other hand, God puts His Holy Spirit in us as the pledge, that we may know that whatever God will give us is guaranteed. One can see that these two aspects are different. On the one hand, the Holy Spirit causes God to know that we belong to Him. On the other hand, His Holy Spirit causes us to know that we belong to Him. We have already seen the Holy Spirit as the seal; now, we want to see the Holy Spirit as the pledge.

Let us read Ephesians 1:14, which says, "Who is the pledge of our inheritance." When we believed in the Lord Jesus, God promised us that He would give us the incorruptible inheritance in the heavens. How do we know that God would not change His mind and take it back? We know that God will not withhold it from us because He gave the Holy Spirit to us as a proof or pledge. The word "pledge" in the original language means a deposit. Originally, I should pay someone twenty thousand dollars, but I first pay him two hundred as a deposit. A deposit means giving someone a little today and a large sum in the future. Have you ever paid or received a deposit when you bought or sold something? When you rented a house, did you ever pay a deposit? Originally, one should pay thirty dollars a month to the landlord, but he first pays five dollars as a deposit for the house. When he gives the five dollars, he is saying to the landlord that the other twenty-five dollars will definitely come. God said that He will give you the incorruptible inheritance in the heavens. How do we know that we will definitely obtain that inheritance in the future? How do we know that we will not lose it? This is because the Holy Spirit has been given to us. The Holy Spirit is the earnest money, the collateral, the pledge, and the token deposit given to us by God. When God gives us the Holy Spirit, He is telling us that all the inheritance in the heavens will be ours in the future.

If a person were to lose his salvation after his believing in the Lord Jesus, what would he do with God's collateral? For instance, I have a house which rents for fifty dollars a month. A brother comes to rent it by first putting down five dollars. This is short of forty-five dollars. He says that the forty-five dollars will surely be given to me. If after a while he does not give me the forty-five dollars, what should I do? I would confiscate his five dollars. However, God cannot do this. First, the promise God has given us cannot fail. Even if God had not given us the deposit, as long as He has spoken, He will fulfill it. Even if God does not give us a pledge or a deposit, when He says that He will give us an inheritance, He will surely keep His word. Because our mind is full of legality, God gave us the Holy Spirit as the proof for us to know that God has given us the deposit. Since we have the deposit, will He not give us the inheritance?

There is a wonderful portion in the Old Testament. Genesis 24 shows us the old servant of Abraham seeking a wife for Isaac. The servant brought with him a lot of riches and precious things from Abraham's house. After he had settled with Rebecca concerning her marriage to Isaac, he gave all these things to Rebecca as engagement gifts. On the one hand, the old servant gave her all these, such as what was on her nose, fingers, head, neck, and hand, to adorn her. On the other hand, all these things were an indication to Rebecca that they were only a little token, that eventually all of Isaac's possessions would be hers.

After we are saved, due to our unbelief, we may think that God did not have the intention to save us. We wonder what would happen if salvation were merely God's toy for us, which, after a few years or a few decades, may be lost and we may become lost again. God is concerned that there may be doubts in our heart. He puts the Holy Spirit within us as the proof to assure us that He will definitely give us the inheritance. My friends, when we look at the Holy Spirit within us, we will realize that we definitely will obtain the eternal inheritance. If God is not going to give us the future inheritance, why did He give us the Holy Spirit? If God is not going to give us the future inheritance, the pledge of the Holy Spirit is meaningless. Our salvation cannot be lost, because the Holy Spirit has been given to us as the pledge. As long as this Holy Spirit is with us, we are saved. The Bible says that He will be with us until the day of redemption. Therefore, we can say assuredly and with concrete proof that we will obtain the future inheritance.

THE BELIEVERS BEING THE GIFTS GIVEN BY GOD TO THE LORD JESUS

Seventh, there is another reason why we will not lose our salvation. In the Bible we see that a relationship exists between the Lord Jesus and God, and a relationship exists between the Lord and us. Many Christians have not clearly seen the relationship between God, the Lord Jesus, and us sinners. Therefore, they misunderstand and think that they can lose their salvation. There is a wonderful word in the Bible that says we Christians, the saved sinners, are the gifts given by God to the Lord Jesus (John 17:6). The Father is here, and the Son is also here. The Father gave the saved ones as gifts to the Lord Jesus. If God has given us as gifts to the Lord Jesus, is there the possibility for us to lose our salvation? We have to consider the matter from two angles.

First, God gave us to the Lord Jesus as a gift. If we were to perish and lose our salvation, if our salvation were not eternal, God's giving us to the Lord Jesus would become a joke on the Lord. This is like a mother giving soap bubbles to her son. Have you ever played with soap bubbles? One dips a tube into soapy water, blows on the tube, and out come the bubbles. We know that those bubbles will disappear in a few minutes. But when the son sees it, he will be thrilled; he will think that the ball is great fun. He does not know that it will break after a little while.

If God were not omniscient, it might be possible for us to perish because God would not know whether our salvation would be temporary or permanent. But God is omniscient; He knows whether we will be saved eternally or temporarily. If God were not omniscient, it could be possible that He would give us as a soap bubble to the Lord Jesus. But if God is omniscient, He would know that after three or five years, that bubble would break. If He were to do that, He would simply be giving air to the Lord Jesus; He would not be giving a gift to Him. God is an eternal God; whatever He does is eternal. If God gives us as a gift to the Lord Jesus, He cannot regard that as a token favor only.

Second, for God to do this would cause a problem to the Lord Jesus also. Suppose God gave us to the Lord Jesus, but three or five years later we perished and lost our salvation. To us, we would have lost it. But whose fault would it be that we lost it? You could blame the gift given by God for being corruptible. But you could also blame the Lord Jesus for not being able to take care of it. Many times people have sent me some very good gifts. When I was away from home, I lost one of them, or damaged them. Either I can blame the gift for being poor, or I can blame myself for being careless in keeping it. God told the Lord Jesus that He gave those people to Him. What would happen if one day those people were to become lost? We cannot blame only God for giving the Lord Jesus a token favor, but we have to also blame the

Lord Jesus for not being able to keep those whom God had given Him.

In John 17:6, the Lord Jesus said to the Father, "I have manifested Your name to the men whom You gave Me out of the world. They were Yours, and You gave them to Me, and they have kept Your word." All the saved Christians are given and awarded by God to the Lord Jesus. Verse 9 says, "I ask concerning them; I do not ask concerning the world." The Lord Jesus did not pray for the world, but "concerning those whom You have given Me, for they are Yours." Hence, we Christians are the gifts given by God to the Lord Jesus. Verse 12 says, "When I was with them, I kept them in Your name, which You have given to Me, and I guarded them; and not one of them perished, except the son of perdition." In the Lord's prayer, He said that He kept every one of those whom God had given Him. There was only one son of perdition. He was Judas. Judas never believed; from the beginning he was the son of the enemy and was never saved. The Lord Jesus said that except for Judas, not one of the ones God had given Him perished.

My friends, you have to know that God has already given you to the Lord Jesus; He has already given you away. This is like a girl being given in marriage. When we were saved, God had given us to the Lord Jesus already. Therefore, all those whom God has given to the Lord Jesus, who have believed in the Lord Jesus, will be kept by the Lord Jesus. The Lord Jesus said, "I kept them in Your name, which You have given to Me." How could a Christian lose his salvation again? After God has given you to the Lord Jesus, how could you vanish away? The Bible says that not one of those whom God has given to the Lord Jesus would perish.

God has given so many of us to the Lord Jesus. Think about it: After God has given all of us to the Lord Jesus, could we perish again after three or five years, simply because we are not good? You should listen to what the Lord Jesus said in 6:37: "All that the Father gives Me will come to Me, and him who comes to Me I shall by no means cast out." Why did you believe in the Lord Jesus? Why did you come to Him? You came to the Lord Jesus and received Him because God gave you to the Lord Jesus. "All that the Father gives Me will come to Me." In other words, all those who come to the Lord are given to Him by the Father. The only reason that you come to the Lord Jesus, that you receive Him as Lord, that you trust in His redemptive work and in His resurrection as your proof of justification, is that God has given you to the Lord Jesus. In heaven God gave you to the Lord Jesus, and on earth you believed in Him and came to Him. God gave you over so that you would come to the Lord Jesus. What does it say after this? "Him who comes to Me I shall by no means cast out." There is no way for us to lose our salvation because God has already given us to the Lord Jesus.

This is not all. There is another portion in the Bible, John 10:29, which says, "My Father, who has given them to Me." Who are the sheep of the Lord Jesus? We are the sheep. In the Gospel of John, we are shown numerous times that we are the gift given to the Lord Jesus by God. God cannot give us away as a token favor that has no substance to it, and the Lord Jesus cannot simply throw us away after He has received us. Do not think that our salvation is a small thing. Since we are not saved by doing this or that, neither can we be unsaved by doing this or that.

I thank God that formerly I was a sinner. I, Watchman Nee, was not asking to be saved. I rejected and opposed Him. But unexpectedly, God brought me through and caused me to accept the word which I had formerly rejected. God took me and gave me to the Lord Jesus. Once I was given, I no longer had any way to escape. When God gave me to the Lord, I received Him as the Savior. From that day on, I was in the Lord's hands. Since we have been given by God and received by the Lord Jesus, how can we escape? If it were we working by ourselves, and if it were we trying and striving to save ourselves, a little negligence or carelessness and we would be through. But we must realize that it is God who has given us to the Lord Jesus and who has saved us.

Let me give you a somewhat imperfect illustration. We know that recently Szechuan had a very severe famine. I read many reports concerning it. Children two years old, who could not even talk yet, were stretching forth their little hands to beg. They begged for food and clothing and maintained their livelihood through begging on the street; they had no other way to go on. Suppose there was a rich person who had plenty of food and clothing at home. If I delivered one of these children over to such a person, in reference to the material things, the child could be said to be saved. Once I give the child over, he is saved. In the same way, we the sinners were dead in sin and perishing. But as soon as God gave us over to the Lord Jesus, we were saved. To be saved means to be given over by God. While we were dead in sin and were waiting for judgment under condemnation, God gave us over. As a result we are saved. This has nothing to do with you. Since God has received you, He could not forsake you again. You were a lost person. You had neither food nor clothing. God gave you to the Lord Jesus, and He received you. How could you be cast out again now? There is no way it can be done. God has given, and the Lord Jesus has received. The Lord said that whoever comes to Him will not be forsaken. Whoever is given to Him by God will not be forsaken by Him. Hence, there is no way for such a one to perish. If you were able to perish, it would mean that God would not be consistent. God has already given over; and the Lord Jesus has already received. How can you perish? It would be a miracle if it were again possible for you to perish. I can say to God, "God, I thank You. I was a sinner; I was dead in sin. While I was yet a sinner, I had no desire to be saved. But You gave me over, and the Lord Jesus has received me. Once You have given me over, and He has received me, I cannot help but be saved."

The Lord Jesus said, "Him who comes to Me I shall by no means cast out." The phrase "by no means" in the original language is very emphatic. It means regardless of anything. "By no means" is a strong expression, but because of our familiarity with the words, we do not pay so much attention to it. It means regardless of any reason, the Lord will not forsake us. There is absolutely not a single Christian whom He has forsaken. We are saved because of the Lord Jesus; we can continue in our salvation and be preserved in our salvation also because of the Lord Jesus. If we think that salvation is of the Lord but that preservation is of ourselves, we will discover that no one can preserve himself for even a single day. I am putting aside man; I am putting down man, but I am exalting the Savior. Everything is accomplished by Him. This is a gift; it is a present. We will never be forsaken.

THE LORD JESUS BEING OUR HIGH PRIEST

Now we come to the eighth point. It is precious to know from the Bible that the Lord Jesus is our offering, but it is more precious to know that He is our High Priest. Many times I asked the brothers and sisters in various places what we would do if the Lord Jesus were not our Savior. Many said that we would be hopeless. If the Lord Jesus were not our Savior, we would be through; there would be no way for us to be saved. Then I asked what would happen if the Lord Jesus were not our High Priest. Many said that this would not make much difference. They think that it would not make much difference if the Lord Jesus were our High Priest or not. We have to know that there is not such a thing. We can keep our salvation only because the Lord Jesus is our High Priest before God. There is no need to mention the former sins or yesterday's sins. The sins that we have committed today alone are enough to cause us to perish. We can continue being saved only because the Lord Jesus is praying for us. The intercession of the Lord Jesus keeps us being saved. Hebrews 7:25 says, "Hence also He is able to save to the uttermost those who come forward to God through Him." Why can He do this? "Since He lives always to intercede for them." The Bible clearly tells us that the Lord Jesus is able to save to the uttermost those who come forward to God through Him. Some people may tell us that we may lose our salvation or that we may still perish. If this were the case, where would you put the prayer of the Lord Jesus? God says that the Lord Jesus lives always to intercede for us. He continues to live to intercede for us.

Who can comprehend all the effectiveness of the intercession of the Lord Jesus for us? If we have a friend who is not saved and we pray for him, God can save him. How much more can the Lord Jesus, who is always before God interceding for us, keep us saved forever! Suppose you have a friend who fell away after believing in Jesus. You prayed for him and wrote letters to him with the hope that he would be a good Christian again. God heard your prayers. After a few years, he was revived. Now would not the continuing, eternal, and lasting prayer of God's Son, the Lord Jesus Christ, who is always before Him, be much more effective? Because the Lord Jesus is the perpetually living High Priest who intercedes for us before God, surely we will be saved by Him to the uttermost.

I am very happy about one thing. Others may forget to pray for me, but I am still a person being prayed for. Man can give up praying for me, but I am still a person being prayed for, because the Lord Jesus always prays for me. I have One who is the High Priest before God. Although man may forget, He never forgets. He lives perpetually as the High Priest to intercede for us.

The Lord Jesus told us that His prayer is for all those who believe; it is for all those who belong to Him. It is not for those in the world. John 17, which we have just read, is quite clear. Verse 9 says, "I ask concerning them; I do not ask concerning the world." "Them" refers to those given to Him by the Father, as mentioned in the previous verses. "I do not ask concerning the world, but concerning those whom You have given Me." Here we see the scope of the Lord's prayer; it is for those who believe in Him and not for the world. There is another matter which we can mention here in passing. The Father is related to the world; and the Son is related to the church. The New Testament never says that Christ loves the world; one only sees that God loves the world. On the other hand, one sees that Christ loves the church and gave Himself for her. The realm of the Father is the world, and the realm of the Son is the church. He said that He did not pray for the world. The effect of His work causes the world to be saved; yet His prayer, His priesthood, is only for Christians. It is not for outsiders.

He prays for us. What is the purpose of His praying for us? He prays for God to keep and protect us so that we can be like Him, so that we can be separated from the world, and so that we can be one. Regardless how strong the world is, how severe the temptations of Satan are, or how intense man's flesh is, the prayer of the Lord Jesus constitutes all the strength; He is able to keep us. If God were not a God who listens to prayer, nothing would happen. But God is One who listens to prayer. In John 11 the Lord Jesus said, "Father, I thank You.... You always hear Me." If God continues to listen to prayer, it will be impossible for us not to be saved. Friends, before you could perish, you would first have to escape from the prayer of the Lord Jesus. The prayer of the Lord Jesus is the guardrail of hell. If you want to go to hell, you need to jump over this guardrail. If you cannot push away the prayer of the Lord Jesus, and if you cannot get rid of the guardrail of prayer, you have no way to perish. Thank God that the prayer of the Lord Jesus is trustworthy.

Let me cite a very clear example. When the Lord Jesus was on earth, Peter once said very proudly to the Lord, "Everyone can deny You, but I will never deny You." Afterwards, Peter failed. The Lord Jesus told him in advance, "Simon, Simon, behold, Satan has asked to have you all to sift you as wheat. But I have made petition concerning you that your faith would not fail; and you, once you have turned again, establish your brothers" (Luke 22:31-32). Because of this word, Peter was able to rise up again after he failed. Not only was he able to rise up, but he was able to help many others. Many people have risen up even today because of Peter. Peter's turning again was not out of himself. It was the power of the Lord's prayer that was holding him all the time. Later, when he remembered the Lord's word, he wept and repented. All this came about by the power of the Lord's prayer. God listens to the Lord's prayer.

The Lord Jesus never prayed for Judas, because Judas was a perishing one from the beginning; he was not saved. From the first day, he was a perishing one. He never believed in the Lord Jesus; he never acknowledged the Lord Jesus as Lord. He merely called Him Master. Judas was a perishing one. The Lord Jesus could not pray for him. But Peter was a saved person; he was definitely saved at the latest by the time of Matthew 16, when he confessed the Lord Jesus as the Son of the living God.

We should not trust in our own prayer. Rather, we should trust in the prayer of the Lord Jesus. It is not a matter of us praying fervently every day. The question is not how many times we have prayed in the last few days. We need to remember that regardless of how many times we pray, nothing will be effected. It is not our prayer that keeps us saved to the end; it is the prayer of the Lord Jesus that can keep us saved to the end. I do not know how many of us here tonight believe in the power of the prayer of the Lord Jesus. Can you entrust yourself without reservation to the prayer of the Lord Jesus? You may think that Satan's temptations are severe, the world's temptations are strong, the fleshly desires are intense, and Satan's attacks are heavy. I cannot agree with your word. If we look at ourselves, oftentimes we will feel like saying we are finished. After a few more temptations from Satan, we think that our flesh will be out of strength. Many times we feel discouraged and are unable to continue in prayer. At such times, we need to look to the Lord Jesus. He is our High Priest. We have to lift our head and look to Him. We should say, "I cannot make it. I cannot even pray. Yet I will trust in Him. He is my High Priest; He can save to the uttermost those who come forward to God through Him because He lives always to intercede for us." We have to rely on Him. Since we have such a High Priest interceding for us, would it be possible for us to lose our salvation?

GOD BEING THE ONE WHO KEEPS US

I am not saying that we should forget about the difficult passages in the Bible. We will address those passages in the next message. But there are many positive things which are undeniable. Not only do we have the prayer of the Lord Jesus and the functioning of the Lord Jesus as our High Priest; the Bible records many other items besides. Our salvation does not depend merely on our believing, but it also depends on the keeping power of God. It is not we who are keeping ourselves, but the power of God that is keeping us. We are

kept by the same condition that enabled us to be saved. The
condition for receiving is the condition for keeping. It is
impossible to have one condition for receiving and another
condition for keeping. By grace we received God's salvation;
by grace we also enjoy God's preservation. If we say that
salvation is by grace but preservation is by works, we have
never read the book of Galatians.

We have studied the books of Romans and Galatians many
times. Romans talks specifically about sinners; Galatians
talks specifically about believers. Romans says that man cannot be justified by works, and Galatians says that man cannot
keep his justification by works. Romans tells us that sinners
cannot trust in works; Galatians tells us that believers cannot
trust in works. Romans tells us that the sinners' justification
before God has nothing to do with the law and works;
Galatians tells us that the believers' preservation by grace
likewise has nothing to do with the law. Having begun by
the Spirit, should we be perfected by the flesh? Having begun
by faith, should we be perfected by the law? Hence, Romans
is for unbelievers and speaks from the angle of unbelievers.
Galatians is for believers and speaks from the angle of
believers. If the receiving of grace before God is free, the
keeping of salvation before God must also be free. The Bible
shows us quite clearly that it is God rather than we ourselves
who keeps us.

First Peter 1:5 says, "Who are being guarded by the power
of God through faith unto a salvation ready to be revealed
at the last time." The last step of salvation is redemption at
the coming of the Lord Jesus. Salvation can be divided into
three stages. The salvation spoken of here refers to our
redemption at the coming again of the Lord Jesus. Through
faith we are being guarded by the power of God unto
redemption. Are we the ones who hold fast to God, or is God
the One who holds fast to us? Is it we who keep ourselves,
or are we kept by God? The Bible says that it is God who
keeps us. The guarding by the power of God implies that if
I were to become lost, the responsibility would not be mine,
but God's. I speak reverently, that if we were to be lost, more
responsibility would fall on God than on us. However, we

should not have any thought at all that Christians can be loose. We will talk about this issue in the next few messages. The problem today is salvation. Salvation is altogether something to do with God. Suppose I leave a seal with Brother Ma because I have to take care of some matters. If Brother Ma loses my seal, whose responsibility is that, mine or Brother Ma's? It is true that I am partly wrong for trusting in Brother Ma; but the direct responsibility lies with Brother Ma because I have entrusted my seal to him. If I handed myself over to God, and later I were to lose my salvation, indeed I would have made a mistake in trusting God. But the mistake would be directly with God. It would be God who would be wrong. We are preserved because of the power of God. Those who do not know God may say that the power of God would be inadequate to keep us. But all who know God have to bow down and say, "We who are being guarded by the power of God through faith will definitely receive the salvation ready to be revealed at the last time." Peter was quite sure that we will receive it. No matter what happens, we will be fully saved.

Why will we be fully saved? Second Timothy 1:12 says, "For I know whom I have believed, and I am persuaded that He is able to guard my deposit unto that day." Whatever Paul had deposited in the Lord, the Lord would guard unto the day He returns. Therefore, we are saved all the way until that day. Many times I consider what would happen if one day I, Watchman Nee, were to go to hell. My perdition would not be a big thing. However, for God's glory to suffer loss would be a big thing. For me to go to hell and perish would not matter very much, but the loss of God's glory would matter a great deal. My perdition would not be that important. But if I were to perish, God would surely not be glorified; His glory would surely be damaged, because it would indicate that God does not guard well. If I were to perish, that would be because God did not keep me well. On account of God's glory, all those who know God and His keeping power would say that there is no way for them to lose God's salvation. Hallelujah! We have no way to lose it. The Word of God is more than clear in this respect.

Concerning the verses on keeping, the one I like the most is Jude 24-25a. It is more peculiar than any of the other verses. It tells us what the name of God is. The name of God is "Him who is able to guard you from stumbling and to set you before His glory without blemish in exultation, to the only God our Savior." What is God's name? God's name is the One who is able to guard us from stumbling; God's name is the One who is able to set us before His glory without blemish in exultation; God's name is the One who is the only God our Savior. This is our God. What is it to not stumble? It does not say that God will keep us from falling, but that He will keep us from stumbling. To fall is to lie down on the ground. But to stumble is only to make a slip. He says that God can keep us from slipping. Not only can God keep us from falling, but He can keep us from slipping.

No teaching in the Bible can have the sinners as its starting point; all teachings must have the Lord Jesus as the starting point. It would be terrible if sinners were taken as the starting point; but if the Lord Jesus is taken as the starting point, things will be clear. If we take the sinners as the starting point, the problem of sin will become obscure to us. There will be many things that we will not consider as sins. Many filthy matters will be regarded as clean; many matters that are weak will be considered as very strong; many shameful things will be considered as glorious. Even after we have become a Christian, we still consider many sinful things as glorious. With those who know God, there are still many sins which have not been judged. There are still many sins that a Christian considers as glorious. If a believer is unclear concerning the matter of sin, how much more will a sinner be unclear? There are many sins that God has already judged in the Lord Jesus, but that were not manifested as sins to us when we were sinners. Only after we believed in the Lord Jesus have we become clear that those were sins. When we were sinners, we were not clear; only after we believed in the Lord Jesus were we clear. However, even Christians are not trustworthy; there are still many things which they do not see. Concerning the losing of one's salvation, if we consider the matter from man's viewpoint, we will never see anything. If we consider the truths of the Bible from our own viewpoint, everything will become confusing. We may think that one thing is greater than others. It is only when we consider things from the Lord's viewpoint that we will be clear. The question is not whether one is able to keep his salvation. The question is whether or not the Lord Jesus is able to guard his salvation.

The proper view is one which stems from the Lord Jesus. If it is up to us to keep our salvation, we may not even be able to keep it for two hours, much less two days. But if it is the Lord Jesus who does the keeping, even if a righteous person were to stumble seven times a day, he would still be able to get up. It is not we who are able, but God who is able. If we turn towards ourselves, our eyes will be in the wrong direction. The Bible tells us that we should look away unto Jesus, who is the Author and Perfecter of faith. The keeping power is the Lord's and not ours. We can trust in God because it is God who keeps us.

The question today is: What method is God using to keep us? Today we have given our life to God. But how will God keep us until the day of the coming of the Lord Jesus? There is no other way but for God to hide our life together with the Lord's life in Him (Col. 3:3). As I read this verse, I am so overjoyed that I could laugh out loud. Nothing can be better than this verse. I do not know if many Christians know how good this verse is. It is impossible to lose the life that God gave to us, because our life and that of the Lord are already hidden in God.

I remember when I was still an unbeliever, as a student, once I finished writing something very important. I told my schoolmate that it was a very important matter and that I would not sell it even for five thousand dollars. I had to go out for a while, and I asked him to keep it safely for me. I gave him that sheet of paper and left. When I came back, I asked him for the paper. He said that he could not give it to me, because after I had said that it was so important, he soaked it in water and swallowed it into his stomach. He patted his stomach and assured me that the paper was there and that it would never be lost. That day I did not know whether to laugh or to cry about it. That sheet of paper was in his stomach; it would never be lost. But neither would it ever be taken out. It was indeed very secure. What God has done today is something more secure. God has hidden our life together with that of Christ in Himself. Where can we find it now? How could we lose it again? God's life to us could only be lost if God Himself were lost. Thank God that God will never be lost. As a result, the life He put within a Christian can never be lost either. The life of a Christian is securely kept; it is kept in God.

THE PROMISES OF GOD

Besides the nine points covered already, there is still another point. Of the nine points that have been covered, none can be overthrown by you, or even by God. No method or way can overthrow them. Once a person is saved through God's grace, no longer can anyone cast him away. But the Lord Jesus considered this as not good enough; He was concerned that we would doubt His work. For this reason, He gave us promises to purposely show us that we will not be lost. We all remember John 10. This portion of the Scripture shows us clearly what our destiny hinges on. Our destiny does not hinge on ourselves; rather, it hinges on the Lord Jesus and the Father.

John 10:28-30 says, "And I give to them eternal life, and they shall by no means perish forever, and no one shall snatch them out of My hand. My Father, who has given them to Me, is greater than all, and no one can snatch them out of My Father's hand. I and the Father are one." The word of the Lord here cannot be clearer: "And I give to them eternal life, and they shall by no means perish forever." These words alone are adequate. Here the Lord speaks in such a solemn and definite way that we shall "by no means perish forever." It is just like saying that we shall not be cast away forever, as mentioned earlier. It is also like saying that we will not come into judgment, but have passed out of death into life, as mentioned in John 5:24. These are all absolute words: "And I give to them eternal life, and they shall by no means perish forever." God is an eternal God. Those who do not know God do not know what God has done. If a man knows God, he knows that whatever God does is eternal. God does not ever do anything temporary. God never changes from one time to the next. What God has done is done once for all. God will not change after two days. Once God has done something, it is done forever. God will not save you today and cast you into hell tomorrow. He will not save you again the following day and cast you into hell again the day after that. If that were the case, the book of life would not look very nice; there would be deletions and corrections here and there. God is eternal. What He gives to us is eternal life. That is why we can never perish. We need to see that whatever God does is eternal. God will never change after a while. Man can change at will, but God cannot change at will. Once He saves us, we are saved eternally; never again could we be in danger of perishing.

What proof do we have of this matter? "No one shall snatch them out of My hand." The words "no one" in the original text have the meaning of "not any created thing." The Lord says that none of the created things can snatch us out of His hand. "I am a good shepherd; I gave life to My sheep, and My sheep shall never perish." As the Father has given the Lord the sheep, no created thing can snatch them out of the Father's hand. John 10:28 speaks of the Lord's shepherding. Verse 29 makes a turn and mentions the Father. Verse 29 says, "My Father, who has given them to Me, is greater than all, and no one can snatch them out of My Father's hand." The hand mentioned in verse 28 is the Shepherd's hand, and the hand mentioned in verse 29 is the Father's hand. Who is the Father? He says that the Father is greater than all. All things are included in this "all." All the created things, all the angels, all the evil spirits, all the human beings, all the created things in the world, including you and me, are included in this "all." The Lord says that the Father is greater than all. No one can snatch us from His hand. He has a big hand that keeps His sheep. How can they ever be lost again? Only one that is greater than the One who is greater than all could possibly snatch us away.

Some may say, "True, others cannot snatch us away, but

I myself can go out." For one to say this proves that his mind is fallen. He does not know God's Word, and he does not know himself. After a person is saved, if he were to perish, would it be because he himself wants to perish? Or would it be because of the temptation of the world, the seduction of the enemy, and the attack of Satan? For a Christian to perish would mean that lust can snatch man from God's hand; it would mean that the devil and the world can snatch man from God's hand. Man does not go to hell because he wants to go to hell; even sinners themselves do not want to go to hell, not to mention Christians. It is clear that man is dead in sin because of the evil spirits' binding work. Everyone in the world is possessed by demons. All the sinners have demons working in them. If the believers can be snatched from the Father's hand, then the evil spirits are greater than the Father of all creation. Here is a sheep in the hand of the Father of all. If nothing is greater than the Father of all, there is no possibility that this sheep can be snatched away. Moreover, it is impossible even for us to escape ourselves, because even we are part of the all things. The Lord Jesus said, "My Father is greater than all." You cannot put yourself outside of the all things.

Thank God that verse 28 shows us the hand of the Lord Jesus and verse 29 shows us the hand of the Father. Verse 28 tells us about the hand of the Shepherd. This is not a matter of law, nor a matter of curse, nor a matter of mercy, but a matter of the keeping by the Lord's hand. Verse 29 says that the Father's hand is greater and more powerful than all. We should consider ourselves securely held by two hands: the Father's hand and the Shepherd's hand.

Not long after I believed in the Lord, Brother Leland Wang and I went to listen to a message in Jiang Wan. The preacher said that we Christians should be fervent. We should preach the gospel and serve the Lord; otherwise, we would be dropped. After the message, I asked Brother Wang, "When do you think you will be dropped?" He said, "I am afraid that I will be dropped tonight." I said, "Yes, I am afraid that I will also be dropped. If I am dropped, I will go to hell." I further said, "If we can be dropped, what is the use of exhorting people to believe in Jesus any longer?" He agreed, saying, "I cannot even eat tonight." I said that not only would we not be able to eat, but we would not even be able to sleep that night. Those in the world do not know the danger of eternal death; they can still eat and sleep. We know the peril of eternal death; we know that we are like chaff before the wind. How can we not worry? This was my story before I knew about this aspect of the truth.

Thank God that it is my Father who keeps the salvation for me. It is my Lord who keeps my salvation for me. Therefore, I know that I am very secure. Twelve years ago, I was in Southeast Asia. Once I rode a bicycle through a big forest on my way to preach the gospel. In the forest, I saw a big mother monkey carrying many little monkeys stacked up one upon another on her back. They were like the human pyramid seen in acrobatic shows. The mother monkey carrying the little ones was running amid the trees. Every so often, she had to jump from one tree to another with a long distance in between. The mother monkey would jump and grab onto a branch of another tree. After swinging over a little, all the little monkeys on her back would fall onto the ground. The mother monkey would then jump down and let the little ones climb up and pile themselves onto her back again. On that day I watched them there for about two or three hours. They were very intriguing to me.

About two months ago, I was in Kunming. There was a Mr. Lin there who had a cat in his house. That cat gave birth to three kittens. One day I went to Mr. Lin's house, and neither Mr. or Mrs. Lin were there. So I went to see the cats. I played with them and used my hand to pet them. The mother cat took the kittens in her mouth and ran away. None of the kittens were dropped. God's saving of us is not like the mother monkey bearing the little monkeys; we do not have to hold onto Him like the little monkeys holding onto their mother with their strength. If that were the case, and if the branches were a bit softer, a few swings and we would be dropped. God's saving of us is like the cat holding the kittens in its mouth. No matter how He runs, we will not be dropped. This is the keeping of God. If you want to hold on to God, it is too strenuous. In three to five years, or even much sooner, you would be dropped. We thank God that it is God who is holding us.

Finally, let us read Romans 8. Last night we read chapter eight, verse 30. We saw five rings. There is no difference in importance in these five rings. We saw that all those who were justified will be glorified. The glorification here in the original language is in the past tense. God is an eternal God. From God's viewpoint, all those who are justified have already been glorified. Maybe, on your side, you still have to wait for a thousand years for your glorification, but on God's side, in His purpose and His plan, it has already become history. Therefore, He says, "And those whom He predestinated, these He also called; and those whom He called, these He also justified; and those whom He justified, these He also glorified." God has already glorified them, and they have already been glorified. Hallelujah! The history has already been written. How can it be wrong? Your future history has already been written, and there is no way for you to change it. Since God has completed the writing of your future history and the future events, He has determined to accomplish it for you.

Because of this, the beginning of verse 31 says, "What then shall we say to these things?" If all the justified ones will be glorified, "What then shall we say?" We shall say nothing. "If God is for us, who can be against us?" God has already made up His mind. How can man be against it? "He who did not spare His own Son, but delivered Him up for us all, how shall He not also with Him freely give us all things? Who shall bring a charge against God's chosen ones? It is God who justifies. Who is he who condemns? It is Christ Jesus who died and, rather, who was raised, who is also at the right hand of God, who also intercedes for us. Who shall separate us from the love of Christ? Shall tribulation or anguish or persecution or famine or nakedness or peril or sword?" Here God is asking, even shouting to the whole world, "Who shall?" Paul asks "who" four times. "Who can be against us?" "Who shall bring a charge against God's chosen ones?" "Who is he that condemns?" "Who shall separate us from the love of Christ?" Paul knew that there is no possibility for any of these things.

Paul did not say, "Who shall cause us not to love Christ?" We often do not love Christ. Oftentimes our love is shaken because it is drawn off by the world. We may not love Christ, but who can cause Christ not to love us? Whether tribulation or anguish or persecution or famine or nakedness or peril or sword, all of these cannot separate us from the love of Christ.

Verse 37 says, "But in all these things we more than conquer through Him who loved us." It is not through our loving the Lord, but through the Lord loving us. If it is through our loving Him, we are hopeless. If it is through our Lord loving us, then "in all these things we more than conquer....For I am persuaded that neither death nor life nor angels nor principalities nor things present nor things to come nor powers nor height nor depth nor any other creature will be able to separate us from the love of God, which is in Christ Jesus our Lord." This shows us clearly and definitely that once God has given us salvation, it is ours eternally. No one can overthrow this fact. These words are too high, too broad, and too profound.

May God show us that whatever God does, He does it thoroughly. God is the Alpha and the Omega. He never stops until the work is completed.

CHAPTER SEVENTEEN

SALVATION BEING ETERNAL— ARGUMENTS AGAINST IT

(1)

We have seen on the positive side that all the work that God has done and all the grace that He has given us at the time we were saved cannot be annulled by the passage of time. We can boldly say that once we are saved, we are eternally saved. Once God has shown mercy to us, we are eternally under His mercy. Once we have the eternal life of the Son of God, we will never lose it.

Although I am very bold in saying this, we human beings are still human beings. Even today many Christian workers do not see this matter. Because man's heart is filled with the flesh and the law, he cannot understand how God's grace can be so great. It is too incredible to him. It is natural for man to think this way. Man is of the flesh, and the flesh is of the law. The flesh knows only the law; it does not know grace. Anything that originates from the human flesh is of the law. But anything that originates from God, from the Holy Spirit, and from grace, is of faith.

In the world we know nothing about grace and gift. All we know is to barter. All day long, our minds are filled with how much we should work and how much we should get for our work. We think that in order to gain anything, we have to work for it. This is our life. For years, we have bartered away our lives, our time, and our energy. We think that if one is to pay a certain price, he first has to be paid an equal amount. If he has accepted a certain amount, then he has to offer certain things in return. Our life is a life of bartering.

Because this is the way we live, we also think that God's grace and eternal life toward us are in the same principle of bartering. When we hear the clear gospel, we may see the light for a while. At that time, we may realize that grace is free and that it is not a matter of bartering. But this realization seems to happen only at the time we are saved. Many people still have not been delivered from the thought of God's grace as a loan to us. They think that if they do not do well, God will claim back the grace He has given. But if a man knows the Bible and is clear about the ten items of truth mentioned in the previous messages, he has to admit at the very least that there can never be such a thing.

Everyone who knows the Word of God should never doubt what he knows because of what he does not know. Since one has seen clearly the sealing and the pledging of the Holy Spirit, eternal life, the hand of the Lord, the Body of Christ, the temple of God, and the promises of the Lord, he cannot overturn what he knows with problems concerning things that he does not know or understand. We cannot overturn the facts we know. However, there are still things we are ignorant of. What we will do now is to take a look at some of the things that we do not know. We will take a few of the supposedly contradictory arguments—especially the more convincing ones—and consider them one by one.

THE KNOWLEDGE OF ETERNAL SALVATION NOT LEADING ONE TO SIN AT WILL

Before we consider some of the problems in the Scriptures, we have to consider one strong objection and doubt that some men raise. Some think that if a person is "once saved, always saved," such a person will surely sin more freely. This can be considered as the most common and strongest point of objection. If a man knows that he is eternally saved and will never be condemned, will he not become loose, start to commit all sorts of sins, and be bold to do anything? Since this could be the case, is not this kind of teaching very dangerous?

I remember that a man once wrote a letter to Mr. Mackintosh—the one who wrote a commentary on the Pentateuch. In that letter he told Mr. Mackintosh that he had heard a preacher a week earlier preaching on the matter of being a child of God eternally. A young man in the audience said that since such was the case, he could do anything he wanted to now. Within a few days, the young man committed all sorts of sins. The writer of the letter complained that because of the teaching of "once a child, eternally a child," the young people had been damaged. In response to his letter, Mr. Mackintosh wrote, "It is true that once a person is a child of God, he is eternally a child of God. But I doubt whether the young man you mentioned is a child of God in the first place. I have a son. Suppose I were to say to my son that since he is my son, he will be my son eternally. Upon hearing this, would my son be so overjoyed that he would right away smash the window with a stone, break his dishes on the floor, pull off the tablecloth and roll the bowls on the floor, and do all sorts of impolite things before me? Can there be such a person? It is true that when a person becomes a son, he is a son eternally. But he will not act lawlessly just because he is a son. If he acts lawlessly, I doubt if such a one is really a son."

According to the Bible, there is nothing wrong with the preacher's word. But the young man's action is totally wrong. To determine if a teaching is right, we can only judge it by the truth in the Bible; we cannot determine it by man's conduct. As teachers of the Bible, we can only be responsible for telling others what the Bible says. We cannot be responsible for telling others what the Bible should say. We do not have this authority. We know that the Word of God says that once we are a son, we are a son eternally. We do not know to what result this knowledge will lead us. The problem today is that man would not judge God's Word with God's Word. Man likes to drag out someone from the corner and say that since man is the way he is, how can one say that a man is "once saved, eternally saved"? It is true that some believers have failed and are weak. It is also true that some people are false ones. It is true that there are millions of believers who have different experiences. We can only judge them by the truth of the Bible. We cannot judge the truth of the Bible by what others have done. We can only prove them wrong by

334 THE GOSPEL OF GOD

the truth of the Bible. We cannot condemn the truth of the Bible as wrong because of what they have done.

The starting point of a Christian is the Word of God, not man's conduct. Today you may ask me whether you are still saved, because you lied yesterday. I cannot ascertain whether or not you are saved based upon whether your lie was a good lie, a bad lie, a bright lie, or a dark lie. I can only tell you what the truth of the Bible says. If this is not the case, there will be no need of the judgment seat and the great white throne. We can only look at what the Word of God says. We can only judge man's act by God's Word. We can never judge God's Word by man's act. It is God's Word that says once a man is saved he is saved eternally. There is nothing wrong with it. Though it is wrong for man to act irresponsibly because of this word, we still must judge everything by God's Word. God's Word is our complete constitution and our highest court.

OPPOSING ETERNAL SALVATION
DUE TO IGNORANCE OF IT

I once heard an evangelist from Shanghai say that the teaching of "once saved, eternally saved" makes a person irresponsible, loose, and not very watchful. One can only make such a statement because he does not fully understand the Word of God. Only those who do not understand God's salvation can say that a man will be irresponsible and loose because he knows that he is eternally saved.

Such people are ignorant of at least three things. First, they are ignorant of God's way of salvation. They do not know *how* God has saved them. In saying this, we are not talking about the way of preservation, but the manner in which God has saved us. God does not threaten us with going to hell in order to gain our belief in Jesus. He does not scare people into heaven. Man always thinks that if he does not repent of his sins, change a little, and perform meritorious works, he cannot be saved. For this reason, he continues to look for ways to be saved. Is this God's way of saving us? Does God put the question of sin continually before man, threatening him to solve it right away? Does God threaten people with the judgment seat and His wrath, coerce them to do various things, and hold in suspense those who do not know what their future holds, to strive with all their strength? If a man has any knowledge of God, he will say a thousand no's to these questions. Those who do not know God will say that it is a good way to cause man's heart to be in fear and trembling and in suspense, not knowing what lies ahead. But those who understand the salvation of God know that this is an evil tiding from hell. It is not the glad tidings. God said the judgment is over. The problem of sin is solved. God's way of salvation is not to hold us in suspense or to scare us into pursuit. He has never coerced us into holiness, righteousness, and sanctification. He said that all things are prepared. The servants said all things are ready (Luke 14:17); God has prepared everything. Now He is coming to give things to you. However, we have changed things around today. We think that a man can be scared into being good. Please remember that a man can only be scared into fainting; he can never be scared into being good.

Second, those people mentioned above are not only ignorant of the way of God's salvation, they are also ignorant of the content of this salvation. What is salvation? It is not just a matter of God solving our problem of sin by His Son. Salvation not only causes our sins to be forgiven, it also gives us eternal life. God's salvation justifies us, and it also gives us the Son of God, putting Him inside of us. Salvation not only causes us not to be condemned by God, but it has put the Holy Spirit within us. Not only does it enable us to live forever in the future, but it has imparted to us God's nature today. This is the content of salvation. Not only do we have forgiveness and justification, and not only are we not condemned and judged, but we have God's nature, Christ, and the Holy Spirit dwelling within us. As a result, man will spontaneously have a new desire, a new inclination, and a new aspiration. God's salvation adds something new to us.

Some have said that salvation is objective. But there are many aspects of salvation which are subjective as well. Salvation has not only solved the problem of sin before God, it has also solved many other problems inside us. Within us, we now have a new life, a new nature, the Lord, and the Holy Spirit. As this is the case, can we be loose? I am not saying that a Christian will never sin. But I am saying that if a Christian does sin, it is a suffering to him. It is not a joy. If a man thinks that he has received a license and a certificate to sin just because he now knows that he is eternally saved, and if such a one does not feel anything when he sins, has no sense of suffering, I doubt that such a one is a true child of God. I am saying that a person is eternally a child of God only after he has first become a child of God. I am not saying that a person can be a child of God eternally without ever once having been a child of God. The Lord is within us. He forbids us to sin.

Third, a person as mentioned above does not know the issue of God's salvation. For those of us who have been saved by God, there is surely a consequence, a result, and an issue. What is this issue? After a man is saved, can he then break the law just because he is now justified in Christ? Can he now freely transgress the Ten Commandments from beginning to end? Can he now do anything he wants to do? Please read the words of Paul in Philippians 3:6 through 9: "As to zeal, persecuting the church; as to the righteousness which is in the law, become blameless. But what things were gains to me, these I have counted as loss on account of Christ. But moreover I also count all things to be loss on account of the excellency of the knowledge of Christ Jesus my Lord, on account of whom I have suffered the loss of all things and count them as refuse that I may gain Christ and be found in Him, not having my own righteousness which is out of the law, but that which is through faith in Christ, the righteousness which is out of God and based on faith." Paul had righteousness through faith in Christ. He received righteousness through faith in God, and not through the work of the law. Was he then free to do anything and to be irresponsible and loose just because of this? He said that the things which were gains to him he had counted as loss on account of the excellency of the knowledge of Christ Jesus. On account of Christ, he suffered the loss of all things and counted them as refuse. Hence, with every regenerated Christian, mature or immature, there is a desire for holiness, a love for God, and a heart to please Christ. I do not know why this is the case. I only know that this is the issue of salvation. You may reason that because Paul was an apostle, he was therefore able to speak as he did in Philippians 3. Let us now look at the ordinary believers. Second Corinthians 5:14-15 says, "For the love of Christ constrains us because we have judged this, that One died for all, therefore all died; and He died for all that those who live may no longer live to themselves but to Him who died for them and has been raised." Here Paul gave us an answer. A man will not be irresponsible and loose just because God has saved him and Christ has resurrected for him. On the contrary, because of Christ's death and resurrection, a person will live to "Him who died for him and has been raised." While he is living on earth today, he does not live to himself, but to the Lord, who has died and resurrected for him.

Thus, the reason a person can say that he can be loose because he knows that he is eternally saved is due to three things: First, he is ignorant of the way, the process, of salvation; second, he does not know the content of salvation; and third, he does not know the issue of salvation, that is, he does not know what salvation can do for man. If you see these three things, immediately you will see that eternal salvation will not only keep you from lawlessness, but it will also make you godly. Eternal salvation will keep us from looseness and will make us sober.

Peter told us in his letter, "According to His promise we are expecting new heavens and a new earth, in which righteousness dwells" (2 Pet. 3:13). Are we free to be loose now that we know where we are going? In the following verse, Peter continues by saying, "Therefore, beloved, since you expect these things, be diligent to be found by Him in peace without spot and without blemish." Because we know that we will be with Him, we cannot be loose or lawless. If we do not know where we are going, we will turn around in circles. But anyone who has a goal, who knows where he is going, will surely choose the straightest path.

THREE THINGS TO UNDERSTAND IN GOD'S WORD

Now let us spend some time to consider some portions of the Scriptures that seem to speak of perdition after salvation. Before this, we have to know a few things. First, the Word of God has absolutely no conflict with itself. On the one hand, God can never say that His sheep will never perish or lose their eternal life, and on the other hand, tell man that he will perish. Man can say wrong things, but God's work is a work of glory. He can never say anything by mistake. If it is so clear on the positive side, it can never be contradicting on the negative side. The things on the negative side must be concerned with other matters related to God.

Second, we have taken the time to identify these passages. Among them we see both genuinely saved ones as well as false ones. The Lord Jesus had a false disciple, Judas. When Peter was baptizing people, there was a person named Simon who might not have been saved. Paul also met many false brothers. Peter said that there were many false prophets, and John said that many had departed from them and proved to not be of them. Hence, in the Bible, there are the genuinely saved ones and the nominally saved ones. Some are not saved at all. Of course they cannot pretend or cover up forever. If we can clearly differentiate between these few kinds of people, the problems will be solved. But if you mix these different kinds of people together, it is like mixing the tares with the wheat. The result will be much confusion.

Third, many places in the Bible speak of the discipline of Christians in this age and not of eternal perdition. Do not think that because we are eternally saved, there is no such thing as discipline. Indeed, there is discipline. If you fail and have become weak today, God will discipline you. There is a difference between discipline and eternal perdition. One cannot mix eternal perdition with discipline. Many verses, which seem to speak of Christians being lost again, actually speak of Christians being disciplined. Not only is there the question of discipline and the question of falsity, but also the question of the kingdom and of the reward. These few things are fundamentally different. Many times, we apply words for the kingdom to the eternal age, and words concerning the reward to the subject of eternal life. Naturally, this will produce many problems. We must realize that there is a difference between the kingdom and salvation, and there is a difference between eternal life and reward. The way God will deal with us in the millennium is different from the way He will deal with us in eternity. There is a difference in the way God deals with man in the restored world and in the new world. The millennium is related to righteousness. It is related to our works and our walk after we have become a Christian. The millennial kingdom is for the purpose of judging our walk. But in eternity, in the new heaven and new earth, everything is free grace. All who are thirsty may come and drink freely (Rev. 22:17). This word is spoken after the new heaven and the new earth have come.

Hence, in the Bible, free gift and the kingdom are two entirely different things. Eternity and the kingdom are also two entirely different things. One cannot put the two things together. In the coming millennial kingdom, God will reward man in a particular way. God will reward man with his rightful crown and glory based upon his works. But as soon as the kingdom is over and the new heaven and new earth begin, everything becomes a matter of grace. Everyone who trusts in the grace of the Lord Jesus will enter in. There will not be the question of work at all. One's personal walk is related to the question of reward, while salvation and justification for the sinner are related to the work of the Lord Jesus. We must differentiate between these two things clearly. Otherwise, when the Bible speaks of the loss in the kingdom, you might be thinking about the loss in eternity, and when God speaks of reward, you might be thinking about salvation. It is true that man's salvation is eternal. But before this eternal salvation is manifested, God will first manifest the matter of reward in the millennial kingdom. One cannot mix these two things together.

In addition to these things, there is another matter that Protestantism has buried in the grave for a long time. Although some may feel that this is something new, actually it was recorded in the Bible long ago. In the Bible there are

at least three things which must be distinguished one from
another. We have just mentioned two of them, which are the
discipline that a Christian receives in this age, and the loss
of reward in the kingdom. If we fail, we will not only be
disciplined today, but will lose the reward in the kingdom.
However, there is still another thing. In the kingdom, there
is definite punishment. The Bible is very clear concerning
this truth. When a person believes in the Lord and is saved,
it is true that the problem of salvation is solved. It is also
true that the questions concerning the new heaven and new
earth and eternal salvation are settled. But if this one
continues to sin and would not repent, he will not only be
under God's government and discipline today and lose the
reward in the kingdom, he will also suffer some definite
punishment in the kingdom.

Some have told us that to lose the reward is punishment
enough. But the defeated ones will still be punished. The Bible
devotes much space to speak of this. The Bible not only tells
us that Christians may not receive the reward in the kingdom,
it also tells us that if Christians sin and do not repent, they
will receive very heavy punishment in the kingdom. We must
distinguish this matter clearly. The question of eternal salvation must not be mixed with the question of nominal
Christians. The question of eternal salvation must not be
mixed with the discipline of this age. The question of eternal
salvation must not be mixed with the question of losing the
reward in the kingdom, and it must also not be mixed with
the question of punishment in the kingdom. One cannot put
these four distinctions together and make "chop suey" out of
them. If one does that, God's work will become a mixture of
everything that does not resemble anything. If God has made
the distinctions, and we ignore the distinctions, we will end
up with many unsolvable problems.

Today, we will first take away these four things. We will
put aside all the words in the Bible that speak of nominal
Christians, the discipline of the believers, the loss of reward,
and the punishment in the kingdom for the believers. In the
next few messages, we will cover them one by one. What we
will talk about in this message are the verses apart from

these four kinds of cases. We will talk about the verses that seemingly speaks of perdition after salvation.

THE ARGUMENT BASED ON EZEKIEL 18

We will first begin from the Old Testament. Let us consider Ezekiel 18:24 and 26, which say, "But when the righteous turneth away from his righteousness, and committeth iniquity, and doeth according to all the abominations that the wicked man doeth, shall he live? All his righteousness that he hath done shall not be mentioned: in his trespass that he hath trespassed, and in his sin that he hath sinned, in them shall he die....When a righteous man turneth away from his righteousness, and committeth iniquity, and dieth in them; for his iniquity that he hath done shall he die." These two verses can be considered as the main verses in the Old Testament concerning this matter. No other verses in the Old Testament are as important as these. These are the most common and most frequently quoted verses. Hence, we have to devote some thoughtful consideration to these two verses.

Ezekiel 18 never speaks of salvation. It does not say anything about Jesus dying for man, nor does it say anything about believing in the Lord to receive life. It does not say how one takes care of the problem of sin. It does not mention anything about the gospel or about Christ. If one tries by force to apply this passage to the gospel, he is confusing the issue. Ezekiel 18 speaks of God's government. What precedes this passage are things related to God's government. One must remember that things in God's government are totally different from things in salvation. God's government refers to how God works, manages, and arranges things according to His plan and will. If a man does not understand the difference between God's salvation and His government, and if he mixes the two together, he is mixing up God's law court with God's family, the father with the judge. He is confusing the word spoken by the father to the servants with the word spoken to the sons. He is confusing the attitude a man has toward his employees with the attitude he has toward his wife and children. Government is government. Government is not the same as salvation. The difference between government and

salvation is as great as the distance between the north pole
and the south pole.

Ezekiel 18 does not show us salvation. Its subject is how
the Israelites can live on the earth. It does not speak of
eternal life. It speaks of the problem with the body. It does
not deal with the question of perdition for the soul. Rather,
it shows us that if a man does not keep the commandment
of God, he will die early physically. It is a question of physical
existence rather than spiritual salvation. No one can ever say
that a son's teeth should be set on edge just because his
father has eaten sour grapes. If someone sitting next to you
eats sour grapes, you might feel like you can taste that same
sourness in your own mouth. But if a father rebels against
God's Word and sins, it has nothing to do with the son. If
the father has to die, the son cannot be a substitute for him.
If a man sins, he himself should be cut off from God's
promised land. This passage is absolutely on the death of the
physical body. This is what the end of verse 2 tells us. Then,
after these words, from verse 3, chapter eighteen repeats that
those who sin shall die. This is not spiritual death. Rather,
it is what Adam experienced, the death of the body. If a man
sins, his days on earth shall be shortened by God. From
verse 3, this chapter repeatedly tells us who can live on earth
through the blessing of Jehovah. This is the context of the
words preceding verse 24. If a righteous man who was
righteous has now turned evil, he will die. All his former
righteousnesses shall not be remembered. This has absolutely
nothing to do with salvation. It is a matter of God's government. It tells us why God would not let a man live on the
earth. It explains why many people die early. It is a word
concerning the judgment of sin for the Jews. It has nothing
to do with us.

THE ARGUMENT BASED ON MATTHEW 24

Now let us take a look at the New Testament. Matthew
24:13 says, "But he who has endured to the end, this one
shall be saved." When many see this verse, they jump up in
surprise. They think that this verse is surely about salvation
and not about God's government, as we have just claimed.

For example, some would say that since I lost my temper yesterday and did not endure, I am now unsaved. They would say that it is true that a person must believe in the Lord Jesus in order to be saved. But they would also say that a person must endure as well. But if you say this, you are twisting the Word of God. You have cut off the head and the tail in God's Word and have taken a sentence out of context. No wonder we confuse the Word of God! If you would understand the meaning of endurance spoken of in this verse, you have to know what was spoken of before verse 13. You must also know what was spoken after verse 13.

Verse 13 is not speaking about the Christians at all. It is speaking about the Jews. What evidence do we have? First, in the following passage we have the Holy Place, the holy temple, and the Sabbath. All these are Judaic matters. What these verses say is that the Jews should flee to the countryside and should pray that their fleeing would not be in winter or on the Sabbath. When they see the abomination of desolation, that is, the image of the beast in the Holy Place, they have to flee. They should not stay in Jerusalem. If this word is for us, how can we possibly know these things, seeing that we are in Shanghai and the image of the beast is to appear in the temple? Although we do have wireless communication today, what Matthew is speaking about here is a knowledge that comes after actually having seen something. Only one who is as near as those in Jerusalem can see. Hence, this passage refers only to the Jews.

Second, the time in this verse does not refer to the time of the apostles, nor does it refer to the time of the church. The time spoken of here refers to the time of the great tribulation. It refers to the last three and a half years at the end of this age. At the beginning of the tribulation, Antichrist will set up his image in the temple. This passage of Scripture has nothing to do with the church. It refers to the future, not to today. There is no possibility for this to happen today, because Antichrist has not yet come, his image has not yet been set up in the temple, and the great tribulation has not yet started.

Matthew 24 refers to the time of the great tribulation.

344 THE GOSPEL OF GOD

The salvation mentioned here does not refer to the salvation of the soul. Rather, it refers to the salvation of the body. All the things mentioned here have to do with the salvation of the body. All those who understand the Bible know that this is the period of time when Antichrist will set up his image in the temple, forcing men to worship it and putting his seal upon people's foreheads. When all the Jews who worship and serve God see the beginning of the tribulation, they must not worship in that way and must not receive the seal. Because of this, they will suffer much. Many persecutions will come upon them. That is why the Lord Jesus told the Jews to flee when they see the image of Antichrist in the temple. If anyone has things at home, they should not bother to get them. They should hide themselves quickly in safe places. Furthermore, the Lord told them to pray that their flight would not be on a Sabbath (v. 20). The reason for this is that they keep the Sabbath. The women should not be pregnant at that time because it would be hard for them to escape. Woe will be to those who are nursing babies at that time. It would also be better if they did not face winter at that time. They should flee to the mountains or to the countryside with the hope that by chance they would not see suffering, persecution, and affliction. At that time, all the forces of Rome will come upon them like a net. They will suffer many difficulties. Many verses in Revelation show us this matter. These people will be saved if they endure during this great tribulation. Because we are too concerned for the matter of salvation, every time the word *save* appears, we apply it to ourselves. But one cannot apply this word to himself here. If he does, he will be twisting the Word of God. In verse 22 the Lord Jesus said another word: "And unless those days had been cut short, no flesh would be saved." When Antichrist is on earth, no one will be able to escape. Thank the Lord that his day will not be that long. Because of this, there will still be some who can flee. If one endures, he can be saved. Hence, the question of salvation here is not a question of eternal life or death. The nature of the salvation mentioned here has to do with falling into the hands of Antichrist or not.

THE ARGUMENT BASED ON GALATIANS 5

Galatians 5:4 says, "You have been brought to nought, separated from Christ, you who are being justified by law; you have fallen from grace." When many read this verse, they think that, first, one can be separated from Christ, and second, one can fall from grace. Such a one is surely not saved. This understanding is wrong. We have to realize the background in which Paul wrote the book of Galatians. When the clear gospel of God was preached to Galatia, the people there heard it. After this, false prophets came to Galatia to preach the gospel. They did not change the first half of the gospel; they changed the second half. The first half said that man was saved only by trusting in Christ and receiving Christ. However, the second half said that before one believes in the Lord Jesus, he cannot have the righteousness from the law; but after one receives the Lord Jesus, he should have the righteousness of the law. Paul wrote the book of Galatians just to refute them. He argued that as a man cannot have the righteousness of the law while he is yet a sinner, in the same way, he cannot have the righteousness of the law after he is saved. We have seen in the previous few messages that Romans and Galatians are different. Romans says that while we are sinners, we cannot have the righteousness of the law. Galatians says that after a sinner is saved, he still cannot have the righteousness of the law. The subject of both books is not having the righteousness which is of the law. These ones taught that after a man has believed in Christ, is saved, and has eternal life, he has to have the righteousness of the law. The first thing and the minimum requirement of the righteousness of the law is circumcision.

After you are clear about the background of this book, you will know what Galatians is speaking of here. In chapter one Paul said that he marveled that the Galatians were so quickly removing from Him who had called them in the grace of Christ to a different gospel. He marveled that they were so quickly deceived to follow another gospel (v. 6). He also said that if he, an angel, or any spirit came and preached to them a gospel different from what they had received, they should be anathematized. The word *anathematize* is the strongest word of curse in the Greek language. It means that all the curse in heaven falls on the cursed one and that all the blessings are withheld. Paul said that his gospel was revealed to him by God alone. He received it in the wilderness of Arabia. This is the reason that his gospel could not contain any mistake. Galatians 2 tells us what this gospel is. In this chapter Peter pretended. When he saw the Jews coming in from James (vv. 11-12), he maintained himself as a Jew. Paul rebuked him to his face. Circumcision means nothing. Christ has already died. It is no longer we who live, but Christ who lives. Chapter three tells us that God's goal is not the law but the promise. The reason that God gave man the law was to cause man first to know his sin and then to accept the Son of God. Chapter four brings out two other things to show us that it is useless for man to keep the law even if he is able to do it. Hagar represents the law, and Sarah represents grace. Hagar must go before Sarah can remain. Even if you can keep the law, you are just Hagar, and you still have to go. The first sentence in chapter five is, "It is for freedom that Christ has set us free." Christ has brought us into freedom. We must now stand firm in this freedom. Do not lose this freedom. If a man keeps circumcision, Christ will be of no benefit to him. If the system of the law is retained, Christ will have to be denied. One cannot keep the law a little and then ask Christ to make up the rest. Christ never does this kind of piecemeal work. Hence, Paul said, "And I testify again to every man who becomes circumcised that he is a debtor to do the whole law" (5:3). Why would some not choose other things in the law? Why would some only pick up the matter of circumcision? Why would they only pick up what they liked and not keep the whole law? If they wanted to keep one item of the law, they would also have to keep the entire law. If one stays, all have to stay. They cannot choose one and reject all the others. Verse 4 says, "You have been brought to nought, separated from Christ, you who are being justified by law; you have fallen from grace." To be brought to nought from Christ means the same thing as Christ profiting nothing at the end of verse 2. It seems as if Christ is not expressed in you. You do not have forgiveness, joy, and peace. Furthermore, if you follow the law, Christ will be brought to nought in you. Here, it is not a matter of receiving salvation. It is speaking of the condition to be saved. Suppose a brother comes to me and says, "Mr. Nee, I should keep the Sabbath. If I do not keep the Sabbath, my salvation will not be complete." I know that this brother is indeed saved. There is no question about it. Now that he has received such a wrong teaching, I must tell him, "If you keep the Sabbath, the work of Christ will have no effect on you. It is of faith that we are in Christ. Now you have gone back to the law. You have fallen from grace." Thus, it is not a question of salvation or perdition. It is a matter of the condition for being saved. It shows us that a man is saved by Christ and not by himself. If a man keeps the law, there will be no grace.

We know that sin leads to perdition. But we must realize that the book of Galatians is not on the subject of sin. The book of Galatians speaks of good works. It speaks of keeping the law of God. Galatians is on the keeping of the law and circumcision. Paul did not say that they had fallen into sin. He said that they had fallen from grace. There is a big difference between the two. To be fallen from grace and to fall into sin are two entirely different things. To be fallen from grace is to be fallen from the principle of grace and to follow the principle of works once again. Today, there are numerous saved believers who have fallen from grace. But they have not lost their salvation. Even we ourselves are the same. A countless number of times we think that we are through. But our salvation is because of the grace of the Lord Jesus.

Paul said that those in Galatians 5 strove to overcome, but they had fallen from grace to trust in their works instead. They wanted to have good works, but when they did this, they fell. What is to be in grace? Grace means that we are lowly and helpless persons. We can do nothing. We have received grace before God. We are in a lowly position. We are looking to God to give us grace. As such, we are those that live in grace. It is not a matter of sin or evil conduct here. If a man trusts in his own work, he is obstructing the grace of Christ. Paul rebuked the Galatians here for following the law after they were saved. They had fallen from grace. He reprimanded them for not having received enough grace and not having received enough mercy from God. To receive mercy and grace from God is to allow God to work. This proves that the flesh is incapable and cannot do anything. We can work by our flesh. But those in the flesh do not please God.

Suppose Brother Yau is an unprincipled man. Every day he earns a dollar fifty cents but spends two dollars. Tonight I have pity on him. He is short of fifty cents. I give him sixty cents. He is like this every day, and I have pity on him also every day. Suppose one day Brother Yau starts thinking, "Mr. Nee has had pity on me and has sent me money every day. But I have to think of a way to discipline myself a little." When he does this, he is doing what the Galatians were doing with circumcision. They were doing it in the flesh, and as a result, they had fallen from grace. I have met such people. From the world's point of view, I like such people. They do not want others to feed them the rest of their lives. They want to be independent. This is good. But the Bible says that, as far as God is concerned, this is wrong because such people have fallen from His mercy. Paul was not rebuking them for sinning. Paul was rebuking them for doing good. Paul rebuked them for doing good because their doing good meant that they did not need God's mercy anymore for the rest of their lives. They would not live in God's mercy anymore.

My friends, man's thought is totally different from God's thought. We think that we can please God by doing a little. But God is happy when we remain in His grace. He repeatedly says that He desires mercy and not sacrifice (Matt. 9:13). Mercy is for God to give you something, and sacrifice is for you to give something to God. God desires mercy. This means that He likes to give things to you. He does not desire sacrifice. This means that He does not want you to give things to Him. If God can give things away, He will feel happy. This is salvation. Salvation is not to make us happy. Salvation is to make God happy. God likes to keep giving. He wants to work continually on us. He wants to give us grace. You might think that it is enough. But He thinks that it is not enough.

You are a poor man and can get by with a few pennies a day. But now you are given a few dollars. No wonder you would think that it is too much. If God is to do something, He wants to do it to the uttermost. If you allow Him to do only a little, He will not feel happy. If you want to be saved, you have to willingly allow God to work. You have to ask God to be merciful to you. God can only be happy if He is allowed to work this way. If you keep trying to give God something, He will not feel happy. When God sees you being shown mercy, He is happy. This is why I say that God desires mercy and not sacrifice.

Galatians 5:4 says that we should not fall outside of grace. It does not say that we should not fall into sin. What is contended here is not the question of salvation, but the question of enjoyment. Before God, we need not move, and we need not keep the law. We do not have to do anything. We should just allow God to work on us and to give us grace. Once we have works, we are fallen from grace. Hence, to say that one has fallen from grace does not refer to the question of salvation and perdition. To be fallen from grace is a question of whether or not we enjoy Christ's benefits for us. To be fallen from grace is a matter of whether or not one allows the work of Christ to operate in him. We thank the Lord that salvation means to be continually under God's mercy and to be continually under His grace.

CHAPTER EIGHTEEN

SALVATION BEING ETERNAL— ARGUMENTS AGAINST IT

(2)

NO TEACHING CONCERNING ETERNAL DEATH IN THE OLD TESTAMENT

In the last message we read Ezekiel 18. Here let me add a few additional words. All those who study the Old Testament carefully and who understand the Old Testament know that it does not have the teaching of eternal death, nor does it have anything like eternal punishment. All the deaths mentioned in the Old Testament refer to the death of the body, and the only place that people go after they die is Hades, and not hell. Two or three places seem to speak of hell. But they are either wrong translations or should be interpreted otherwise. All the deaths mentioned in the Old Testament are the death in the body. They are not eternal death. The Old Testament was written to the Jews. Because they were earthly men, their failures were also earthly failures, and their punishments, earthly punishments.

I am not saying that there is no such thing as eternal death in the Old Testament; there is such a thing in the Old Testament. But the Old Testament never teaches us about eternal death. In the Old Testament, those that were blessed by God had much cattle, sheep, gold, and silver bestowed upon them. These were the signs of God's blessing. But in the New Testament, those who are blessed by God can say, "Silver and gold I do not possess, but what I have, this I give to you: In the name of Jesus Christ the Nazarene...walk!" (Acts 3:6). In the Old Testament, there were the gold and the silver. In the New Testament, there is no silver or gold. The Old Testament, though not exclusively dealing with things in the flesh, mainly speaks of the physical and material aspect of things. In the Old Testament, when a man was blessed by God, he would enjoy long life, have many offspring, and have much wealth. These are the blessings of the Old Testament. But in the New Testament, we do not see these things. On the contrary, we see that James died. Stephen died. Many were martyred for the sake of loving the Lord. They were not at all cursed. Moreover, the New Testament never made offspring an item of blessing. On the contrary, those who live for the Lord should remain virgins. Hence, what the Old Testament shows us and what the New Testament shows us are two entirely different things.

This does not mean that in the Old Testament there is no such thing as eternal death. But this is not taught as a teaching. Because man does not understand this truth, the New Testament tells us about eternal death. In the Old Testament are a few places that seem to speak of eternal death, but are wrong translations. One of them is translated as the wicked being turned into hell (Psa. 9:17). But actually it should be translated as the wicked going to Sheol. It is temporary, and it is not for eternity. In Isaiah 66:24 it mentions worms which shall not die and the fire which will not be quenched. It seems that this is speaking of the same thing that the Gospel of Mark speaks of (Mark 9:48). But please remember that Isaiah was not saying that unless the Israelites repented they would go down to hell, where the worm will not die and the fire will not be quenched. Isaiah was prophesying concerning a group of people who will go to hell at the end of the millennium, where the worm will not die and the fire will not be quenched. Isaiah was not speaking of eternal death at all. If we drag him into the subject of eternal death, we are trying to import something foreign. This would become an imported item.

CHRIST OF NONE EFFECT
BEING DIFFERENT FROM SEPARATION FROM CHRIST

One thing more we have to know. Galatians 5:4 says, "You

have been brought to nought, separated from Christ, you who are being justified by law; you have fallen from grace." In the original language the word "brought to nought" is *katargeo*. This is a passive verb. There is a little of the sense of separation. *Kata* has somewhat the sense of detachment, but the sense is not very strong. The word *katargeo* means to be led away from the effect and the function. Stephan's lexicon of Greek words can be considered as one of the best. It tells us that the word here means to be led away from the function. One must see the difference between separation from Christ and being led away from the effect of Christ. These are two different things. If a man has left Christ and is separated from Him, then everything is through. But this is not what Paul was saying here. Paul said that if they keep the law, they have fallen from grace. If they want to hold on to the law, they have to let go of grace. If they follow the law, they will lose the effect of Christ.

What is the effect of Christ? If the effect of Christ is manifested in me, I can rejoice. Though I may be weak and worthless, I know that His grace is sufficient for me, and my heart is able to be at peace. This joy and peace that I have in my heart is the effect of Christ on me. This is Christ working out His effect on me. I do not try to be saved by my works. I know that I am saved already. I do not have to strive to be saved. I do not have to plead desperately. Nor do I have to struggle. I can rest in His work. This is the effect of Christ. Today many Christians have turned away from Christ. Christ does not have much effect on them.

Suppose I owe someone a great deal of money. I cannot repay it even if I were to sell all that I have. Now I have a best friend. He says that since I am so heavily in debt, he will write a check for me so that I can clear my debts. But I am a lazy man. I am too lazy to cash the check. Now do I have money at home? I do, but I also have a debt at home. I have the check, but the check has no effect on me. The debt is still there; it has not been repaid. I am still bearing the burden of the debt. Today God has given us the check already. But we have not cashed in on the effect of this check.

Hence, to be separated from Christ and to have Christ

made of none effect on us are two different things. To be
separated from Christ is to be not saved. But we can never
be separated from Christ. Romans 8 tells us that there is no
way for us to be separated from Christ. It says that no one
can separate us from the love of Christ. The grace we receive
from Christ and the blessing we have from God are ordained
by God. No one can overturn them. They cannot be overturned,
because they are based on righteousness. Through the many
things that Christ has accomplished for us, the problem of
eternal life and death is solved. There is no way to overturn
this, for this is based on righteousness. But on the subjective
side, the absence of peace in the heart and the continual
presence of unhappiness is a Christian problem. A man may
worry about how he can receive grace and how he can preserve
his salvation. Every day his heart is held in suspense, not
knowing what he should do. When a man has turned away
from the effect of Christ, he will not receive the effect he
should receive from Christ. Hence, Galatians 5:4 shows us
that for a man to pursue after law is for him to fall from
grace. When he falls from grace, he is away from the effect
of Christ. Therefore, this does not refer to man's losing his
salvation after he is saved. Rather, it refers to one's not having
the joy and peace of salvation.

THE ARGUMENT BASED ON 1 CORINTHIANS 8:11

In this message, we will consider a few more verses. First
Corinthians 8:11 says in the King James Version, "And
through thy knowledge shall the weak brother perish, for
whom Christ died?" This verse presents a problem. This
person mentioned here is definitely saved, for he is called a
brother. It is true that he is a weak brother. But nevertheless
he is a brother, a person who belongs to the Lord. But here
it says that he could perish. The word *perish, apollumi,*
carries two meanings in the original language. One can be
translated as perish. The other can be translated as destroy.
But this word is the same as the word *perish* used in John
3:16. John 3:16 says that everyone who believes in Him shall
not *apollumi,* but have eternal life. If we can use the word

destroy in 1 Corinthians 8:11, then we can translate John 3:16 as destroy also. Here then is a problem.

When we read the Bible, we cannot read it in a superficial way. We have to study the context in detail. Only after reading the context carefully can we know what the verse says. One cannot hear clearly what others are saying by leaning the ear against someone's window. One of the most foolish things on earth is to listen to others through the keyhole behind closed doors, for one may not catch what is spoken before or after. If you pull a sentence out of context from the Bible, you will surely not be able to understand it clearly. To understand it clearly, one must read the context.

The subject of 1 Corinthians 8 is on the forbidding of Christians from eating food offered to idols in the idol temple. The Corinthian believers proposed that it was all right for Christians to eat food offered to idols in the idol temple. Their reason was that there is only one God in heaven and on earth. The idols are nothing. If one offers food to the idols, and the idols are real, then the offerings are real offerings. If the idols are not real, then the offerings are not offerings at all, but are food only. If they are not offerings, what harm is there to eat them? If the idols are not real, then the temples are but non-temples, and it would not mean anything for one to eat the offerings in the temples of the idols. They therefore thought that the offerings could be eaten. This is what the Corinthians said.

But Paul said that the offerings should not be eaten. His reason was not that the idols were real or the temples real. At the beginning of chapter eight, Paul said, "Now concerning things sacrificed to idols, we know that we all have knowledge." The word "we" refers to the Corinthian believers. Because all have knowledge, therefore they can eat. However, "knowledge puffs up, but love builds up." The purpose of love is to build others up, whereas knowledge puffs up. It is true that the Father is God, that Jesus is the Lord, and that the idols are nothing. But there were many weak brothers in the church in Corinth. They did not have the knowledge; their minds were not as keen as yours are. Although you can turn the words around and consider there to be nothing, these ones do not understand the things you are saying. They still think that it is against the commandment of the Lord to do something like this. One has to remember who these people were and what their backgrounds were. Today you may think that idols are nothing. But these ones had offered to idols before, thinking that they were offering to God; they thought that the idols were gods. When you eat, you do not feel anything. But if they eat, they would be reviewing their past sins. They were not like you. You have the knowledge, and therefore you can eat and go away. But they would feel that they were doing the same thing that they had done before and were sinning the same way they had sinned before. In their mind, they still consider this as sin. Hence, for the sake of the other Christians, and for the sake of loving them, though you may have the knowledge, you would rather not do it. You have the knowledge, but they do not have the knowledge. They feel condemned in their conscience before God. They feel that they have committed some great sin and are falling away again. Therefore, for their sake, we would not eat. This is the general meaning of this passage.

First Corinthians 8:4 to 7 say, "Concerning the eating of things sacrificed to idols, we know that an idol is nothing in the world and that there is no God but one. For even if there are so-called gods, either in heaven or on earth, even as there are many gods and many lords, yet to us there is one God, the Father, out from whom are all things, and we are unto Him; and one Lord, Jesus Christ, through whom are all things, and we are through Him. But this knowledge is not in all men; but some, being accustomed to the idol until now, eat the food as an idol sacrifice, and their conscience, being weak, is defiled." Please notice the word *accustomed* here. This was their past habit. Verse 12 says, "And sinning in this way against the brothers and wounding their weak conscience, you sin against Christ." This passage teaches people to refrain from food offered to idols on account of the love for the brothers. You cannot act freely and put your brother into trouble simply because you have the knowledge.

From verse 7 until the end, the problem was that of the conscience. It was not a problem of the spirit. Paul was not talking here about eternal salvation or eternal perdition. Paul was telling us what to do in relation to a brother with a weak conscience. If a man does something that he knows he can do, his conscience will not condemn him. But if he does something that he knows he should not do, his conscience will condemn and rebuke him continually. For example, we know that we do not need to keep the Lord's Day, and we do not need to keep the Sabbath. It is all right to shop and to work on the Lord's Day. Our conscience never condemns us. This is a grace of the New Testament. The Lord has not laid upon us the burden of the Sabbath. But some do not have this knowledge. When they shop on the Lord's Day, they think that they have sinned a great sin. After such a one does this, his conscience will not be at peace. Sometimes the question of sin is simply a question of the conscience. Man's conscience determines for him what his sins are.

Paul was saying that here is a weak brother. Formerly he worshipped idols. Now he sees others eating, and he wants to join them. For you to eat is all right, because you have the discernment and you know that the idols mean nothing. You could therefore freely eat. He eats, not because he has the discernment, but because he sees you eating. All the time he is eating, he has no peace. You eat with joy. He eats with fear. After this meal, he can no longer pray. His conscience tells him that he has just sinned and that he has forsaken God to worship idols just as he used to do. His conscience begins to perish before God. He feels guilty before God. He thinks that he is through and that he has gone back to his former sins again.

In addition to John 3:16, the original word for perish also appears in Luke 13, 15, and 21. But in those three places, this word was used very differently. In chapter thirteen, Pilate had killed quite a number of people and had mixed their blood with their sacrifices. The Lord Jesus told the people that they should not consider these Galileans to be more sinful than they were. Unless they repented, they would all likewise perish. The perishing here refers to the body being killed; it has nothing to do with man's soul. The Lord said that there were eighteen killed when the tower in Siloam fell.

Unless these repented, they would similarly perish. This refers to the killing of the outward body.

In the parable of the prodigal son in Luke 15, the prodigal said, "How many of my father's hired servants abound in bread, but I am perishing here in famine!" Perishing here does not refer to the perishing of the soul. Hence, this word does not refer only to eternal death, but to the killing of the body and to starvation. One can be considered as perishing when he is killed. He can also be considered as perishing when he is starving to death.

In Luke 21 the Lord says that the hair of our head shall by no means perish. Even our hair can perish. Now this cannot possibly mean eternal death anymore. From these three places, one can immediately get an idea of what Paul referred to here. He was referring to something that would cause the conscience of a weak brother to perish. In the meeting he would not be able to pray anymore. He would think that he was through, that he had worshipped idols again and had eaten of the food offered to idols in the idol temple again. He would think that he had left the living God again, and his conscience would be destroyed because of you.

If we read this portion of the Scripture in 1 Corinthians 8 carefully from verse 7 on, we will see why Paul said what he did. "But this knowledge is not in all men; but some, being accustomed to the idol until now, eat the food as an idol sacrifice, and their conscience, being weak, is defiled." Please note that this refers to those whose conscience, being weak, is defiled. "But food will not commend us to God; neither if we do not eat are we lacking, nor if we eat do we abound." This is absolutely our standard: If we eat there is no merit, and if we do not eat, there is no loss. But those without the knowledge have a problem here. "But beware lest somehow this right of yours become a stumbling block to the weak ones." The weakness here does not refer to a moral weakness or a doctrinal weakness. Rather, it refers to weakness in the conscience. If it meant weakness in one's moral condition or doctrine, the verse would lose its meaning. It refers rather to the weakness in the conscience. "For if anyone sees you who have knowledge reclining at table in an idol temple, will not his conscience, if he is weak, be emboldened to eat the things sacrificed to the idols?" Those with a weak conscience think that since others can eat it, so can they. But if such a one eats it, his conscience will be defiled. "And through thy knowledge shall the weak brother perish, for whom Christ died?" (KJV). Hence, the perishing here does not refer to eternal perdition of a saved brother. The perishing here refers to the spiritual stumbling of a brother due to weakness.

If what 1 Corinthians 8 says is that a brother's knowledge can cause another to eternally perish, then I can say that a person's being saved or perishing depends on another's knowledge. If that were the case, I could send every one of you to hell by my knowledge. If that were the case, man's perishing would not be determined by himself, but by some others. We know that there can be no such thing. The Bible says that all who believe in the Lord Jesus will have eternal life. Whether or not a man will perish before God depends on whether he believes in the Lord Jesus. How could others bring me to hell? This is absolutely unscriptural. Concerning the use of the word *perishing,* we can say that perishing here does not refer to the matter of eternal life and death. Rather, it refers to the damaging of the conscience and the bringing of a person under.

Let us go on. Verse 12 says, "And sinning in this way against the brothers and *wounding their weak conscience,* you sin against Christ." The sinning against the brothers here refers to the causing of the weak brother to perish through knowledge in verse 11. The sinning in verse 12 refers to the causing to perish in verse 11. Verse 12 says that when you cause your brother to perish because of your knowledge, you are wounding his weak conscience. Hence, the perishing mentioned in the previous verse refers to the wounding of the conscience. This does not refer to eternal life or eternal death and perdition.

Verse 13 goes on to tell us what it is to wound their conscience. "Therefore if food stumbles my brother, I shall by no means eat meat forever, that I may not stumble my brother." If you put the three verses together, you will see what perishing here means. To perish is to have the brother's weak conscience wounded, and to wound the weak conscience of the brother is to cause the brother to stumble. Therefore, verses 11, 12, and 13 are three rings that are linked together. They show us what perishing is. What is covered here is absolutely not the perishing in relation to salvation. If you insist on explaining it this way, saying that a saved person will perish, you will find this argument hard to support. You will have a hard time explaining it that way.

THE ARGUMENT BASED ON JAMES 5:20

James 5:19-20 says, "My brothers, if any one among you is led astray from the truth and someone turns him back, let him know that he who turns a sinner back from the error of his way will save that one's soul from death and will cover a multitude of sins." Some people also infer from these two verses that a saved person can perish. To them, in verse 19 we have the brother. Then in verse 20, we have the sinner. To them, verse 19 says to turn a brother back, and verse 20 says that in turning back the brother, the soul is saved from death. This would mean that some brothers need to turn back, and some need to have their souls saved from death. Would this not say plainly that a brother can lose his salvation?

In order to understand these two verses, there are a few things here that we have to pay attention to. First, James 5:19 and 20 are like a lone mountain. They are not connected to the preceding verses, and they have nothing to follow. All the other Epistles in the Bible have greetings and benedictions. James is the only book that ends this way. Verses 17 and 18 speak of prayer. All of a sudden these few words seem to break in from nowhere. This is a very peculiar thing.

Second, from chapter one until the end, the book of James is on practical love among the brothers and sisters. Because of love, there is the mercy, the care, and the concern for the brothers. This is what the book of James shows us. From 1:1 to 5:18, there is a continuous line, a definite goal, and a subject. Verses 19 and 20, however, seem to drop down from nowhere. One can say that 1:1 to 5:18 are very organized. But we do not know where these two final verses come from.

Third, in principle, since James 1 through 5 speaks of love expressed in one's conduct, verses 19 and 20 should not deviate from this point. They should also tell us what we should or should not do when we love the brothers. If a sinner continues in the error of his way, and you save him in love, you are saving a soul from death. In addition, you will also cover a multitude of sins. All readers of the Bible know that what covers a multitude of sins is love (1 Pet. 4:8). The many sins spoken of here do not refer to sins before God. They refer to the sins before man. If you turn a sinner from the error of his way, God will no longer remember his sins and will cast them into the deep sea. All his sins will be under the blood. Now what about us? Suppose Brother Yuan was a very evil man before he became a Christian. His past history is very black and unseemly. I know his past history and stories of his past. I could lay them out and expose them. But if I expose his sins of the past, I am acting contrary to God's will. God has cast his sins into the sea. After we are saved, God does not mention our past sins any longer. When I see a brother, I have to cover his past because among us God has covered our past sins.

Verse 20 is on the matter of principle, and verse 19 is on the matter of example. In other words, verse 20 is the formula, the law, and the principle of action, whereas verse 19 is the case study and the individual incident. Verse 20 says that if anyone turns a person, he will not die and his sins will be covered before God and before men. Verse 19 shows us what happens when one brother among us is led astray from the truth or has erred in his way. We have to turn him back. The exhortation in verse 19 is based upon the principle in verse 20. If you see a brother in the church led astray from the truth, you have to recover him. When a sinner is turned, his soul will not die and his many sins will be covered. This being the case, how much more should we do the same on behalf of a brother? What James was saying here was that we should do unto the brothers as one would do unto the sinners. James is telling us here that a Christian should treat his brothers and sisters with love and should recover them. This portion is not speaking of a brother perishing.

THE ARGUMENT BASED ON HEBREWS 6:6

Now we have to consider Hebrews 6:1-8. This passage presents the greatest problem in the Bible. Almost all the ones who doubt that salvation is eternal take Hebrews 6 as their city of refuge. All of them dig their support material from here. They argue that if a man was saved and now has fallen away, it will be impossible for him to be renewed again to repentance. Would that not mean that such a person is through and is doomed to perish? Because many are not clear, they take this passage as reason for man's perishing.

But we have to realize that the subject of Hebrews 6 is not salvation. It has nothing to do with salvation at all. If one wants to understand this passage, he must begin from the end of chapter five. There it says that many who should be eating solid food are still taking milk. According to their age, this group of believers should have been the teachers already. But they were still like babes and were not progressing, but were staying at the same place. Hence, chapter six begins by saying, "Therefore leaving the word of the beginning of Christ, let us be brought on to maturity." The subject of Hebrews 6:1 is therefore progress, and not salvation. If you put the subject of salvation in, surely you will encounter difficulty. The purpose of this chapter is to tell others how to progress, and not to tell us how to be saved. The first thing we must take note of is that the topic here is on progress to maturity, not regressing to perdition.

The apostle was here talking about being brought on to maturity. Verses 1 through 8 can be divided into three sections. We can use three words to represent these three sections. The first section is on having no need, the second section is on having no possibility, and the third section is on having no right. This portion tells the Hebrew believers from these three standpoints that they have to progress. First, they have to leave the word of the beginning of Christ and should not lay again a foundation. The word of the beginning of Christ is like the cornerstone in a building. In building a wall, a person does not need two foundations. The apostle said that these ones had been talking about foundational things. But the foundation was laid already; there was no need to lay the foundation again. The word of the beginning of Christ are teachings such as repentance from dead works, faith in God, baptisms, laying on of hands, resurrection of the dead, and eternal judgment. All these are the words of the beginning of Christ. The apostle said that these need to be done only once. There was no need to do them again. He was exhorting them to go on to perfection.

The second section requires an introduction. Before we read verse 4, let me first tell you about this introduction. Before the apostle wrote verse 4, he anticipated that these ones would ask, "If you say that we should not lay again the foundation, what then should we do if we sin again? If a person has failed, backslidden, and sinned, does he not have to lay again the foundation?" Here the apostle said something in anticipation of their question. "For it is impossible for those who have once been enlightened and have tasted of the heavenly gift...." If you have a Greek New Testament in your hand, you will see that the word *once* according to the grammar of the original language does not refer only to the first item of the list, but to every item in the list. It should read, "...those who have once been enlightened, and who have once tasted of the heavenly gift, and have once become partakers of the Holy Spirit, and have once tasted the good word of God and the powers of the age to come...." This is very clear in the original text. Here is a man who has been enlightened, has tasted of the heavenly gift, and has become a partaker of the Holy Spirit, and has tasted the good word of God and the powers of the age to come. The age to come is the millennium. This one has tasted the powers of the millennium. In other words, he has seen and tasted miracles, wonders, healings, and the casting out of demons. If such a one falls away, it is impossible for him to be renewed again to repentance. "And yet have fallen away...." One British brother who studied Greek and who specialized in the book of Hebrews for his whole lifetime said that the falling away here means to have a slip of the foot. When it says that it is impossible to again renew themselves unto repentance, many think that it means perdition. But this explanation is not valid.

If there is a man who has once been enlightened, who has once tasted of the heavenly gift, who has once become a partaker of the Holy Spirit, who has once tasted the good word of God and once tasted the powers of the age to come, is it possible that such a one cannot any longer repent once he makes a slip? Are there cases of fallen Christians who have risen up again? The Word of God tells us that indeed there have been many, and church history also tells us that indeed there were many. Many Christians who had once slipped eventually became the best runners of the heavenly kingdom course. Beginning from Peter, there have been countless Christians who have fallen and have risen up again. If there were no possibility for these to rise up again, then Peter would have been the first one that could not have risen up. He slipped terribly. We can say that he had fallen flat on his face. Peter was not the only one. Throughout the two thousand years of church history, countless Christians have failed. But eventually they became the best testimonies. I can enumerate countless proofs of this. If what was said before was right, then there should not have been a single one; if there is one, the Bible would be wrong.

In this passage, there is a word in the original text, *palin,* which means again. There is also another word, *anakainizo,* right after this word, which means to renew. Hence, according to the original text, this part should be translated as "once having slipped, it is impossible to again renew to repentance." The apostle was telling the Hebrew believers here that the repentance from dead works, the faith in God, the teaching of baptisms and of the laying on of hands, of the resurrection of the dead and of eternal judgment, are all words of the beginning of Christ. If they have once been enlightened, once tasted of the heavenly gift, once partaken of the Holy Spirit, once tasted the good word of God, and once tasted the powers of the age to come, and have then slipped, they cannot lay again the foundation and cannot again be renewed to repentance.

Please remember that the repentance here is the foundation spoken of in the first section. The repentance here does not mean repentance in general, for in the previous verses there are six items of the words of the beginning of the Christ. The first is repentance from dead works. Hence, we cannot take the repentance we have in our concept and equate it to the repentance here. We must consider the context of the Scripture, and we must expound it according to the thought of the apostle. The repentance spoken of by the apostle is the same as the repentance from dead works in verse 1. The meaning here is that after a man has believed in God and has been baptized, and after he has understood the coming judgment and the truth of resurrection, and has repented of dead works, he cannot repent again for what he has repented of. Once he is baptized, he cannot be baptized again. Once he has believed in the teaching of judgment, he cannot try to believe again. Once he has believed in the teaching of resurrection, he cannot try to believe again. The word repentance here includes all six items mentioned above. The apostle did not repeat the words "to renew again" as many times as I did: to renew again the repentance from dead works, to renew again faith toward God, and to renew again this and that. He only needed to use the words *to renew again* once. If there had never been anything yet, we would use the words *to begin*. But if there was something already, we would use the words *to renew again*. The apostle was afraid that we would not understand the meaning of *renew, anakainizo*. Hence, he added a further word *again, palin*. Hence, the repentance spoken of in verse 6 must refer to the repentance in verse 1. If the repentance in verse 1 were mentioned as the second item, we might not be very clear. But thank the Lord, it is placed as the first item. As long as it is the first item, we know that all the other items are like this one.

The apostle was saying that the word of the beginning of Christ can be compared to the foundation. For one to be a Christian, first there is the need for the repentance from dead works, to judge his sins. Then he has to have faith in God, to be baptized, to have the laying on of hands, and to believe in the resurrection of the dead and the eternal judgment. All these are foundational matters. Once the foundation has been laid, there is no need to lay it again.

While one is building on this foundation, even if his foot slips, there is no need to lay again the foundation. Even if one wants to lay a foundation again, it is impossible to do so. For example, Brother Wu has just come into the meeting hall from the main entrance on Wen-teh Lane. After he came into the alley from the entrance, and as he was turning the corner to come into the building, he slipped. What then should he do? His goal is to come to the meeting. Now he has slipped. He does not need to start all the way from Wen-teh Lane again. He can rise up from where he has slipped. The apostle was saying that once a person has been enlightened and has tasted of the heavenly gift, if he slips, he cannot repent from dead works again, believe in God again, be baptized again, have the laying on of hands again, and believe in resurrection and eternal judgment again. In other words, the apostle has no intention to say that a man can perish again after he is saved. What he means is that after a Christian is regenerated, he cannot be re-regenerated. At most we can be regenerated once. The apostle was not saying that one is not allowed to repent again. He was saying that it is impossible to repent by starting all over again.

The next part of verse 6 says, "Crucifying again for themselves the Son of God and putting Him to open shame." Some have said that to fall is to crucify the Son of God again. Who can crucify the Lord again? The work of the Lord Jesus was accomplished once for all. He was not like the bull and the goat, which must be slaughtered when they are needed. On your side, you cannot renew your repentance. On the Lord's side, He cannot renew the crucifixion. If you have to renew your repentance, that means that the Lord Jesus will have to renew His crucifixion. If that were the case, then you would be putting the Lord to open shame. You would be saying that the Lord Jesus' onetime crucifixion was not enough, that there have to be more crucifixions. Hence, this is not a question of salvation and perdition here.

In the previous messages, we have seen that eternal salvation is a fact that cannot be overturned. If there is a fallen and backslidden Christian among us, who was once clearly saved and was clear about God's salvation, for him to rise up again does not require a fresh start. As long as he would rise up today, that is all that is needed. There is no possibility of crucifying the Lord Jesus again and putting Him to open shame.

In the last section in verses 7 and 8, not only was the apostle saying that there is no need and that there is no possibility, but he went on to say, in a more serious way, that there is no right. Why do we not have the right? It is because a laying again of the foundation would crucify again the Lord Jesus. If one does that, there would be serious danger ahead of him; he would suffer great punishment. "For the earth, which drinks the rain which often comes upon it and brings forth vegetation suitable to those for whose sake also it is cultivated, partakes of blessing from God. But if it brings forth thorns and thistles, it is disapproved and near a curse, whose end is to be burned." We will leave the detailed discussion of this passage until later. After one reads Hebrews 6, he can see that this chapter speaks of the matter of progress. It is not on the question of salvation or perdition. Hebrews 6 never tells us that a saved person can perish.

FOUR THINGS TO BE DIFFERENTIATED

Here we have to consider again the four things mentioned in the Bible. They are the four things that must be distinguished one from the other, which we mentioned earlier. If a man wants to understand salvation, first, he has to differentiate between the genuine Christian and the false Christian. Second, he must differentiate between the discipline of the believers and eternal salvation. Eternal salvation is one thing, and God's discipline of His children is another. It is one thing for a Christian to be chastised in this age. It is another thing for an unbeliever to perish in eternity. A Christian will not perish eternally, but he can be chastised. There are many verses that speak of chastisement for a Christian. One cannot apply these verses to salvation.

Third, there is a great difference between the kingdom and eternal life. In other words, there is a great difference between reward and gift. It is one thing for you to be saved. It is another thing for you to reign, to rule, and to share the glory with the Lord Jesus in the millennium. There are many places in the Bible that speak about a person being removed from the kingdom. Because many are not clear about the difference between the kingdom and eternal life, the reward and salvation, they apply the verses on the kingdom to the matter of salvation. Many think that to be removed from the kingdom means to perish. These, however, are two entirely different things. A Christian can lose his position in the kingdom, but a Christian cannot lose his position in salvation. Although a Christian can lose his position of reigning together with Christ, he cannot lose his position of being a child of God.

Fourth, not only does the Bible say that a Christian will suffer discipline today, and not only does it say that some Christians can lose the kingdom, but there are definite punishments for a Christian in the kingdom as well. The Bible says that many Christians will suffer discipline in this age. They will lose the reward in the coming age and will also suffer punishment. A Christian can lose his reward in the future. He can also be punished with definite, positive punishments. But one cannot mix the punishment in the millennium with eternal perdition. Eternal perdition is one thing. Chastisement in the kingdom is another. When a Christian is chastised, it does not mean that he will perish eternally. Salvation is eternal. Chastisement is only a discipline in the family. If some children cannot be disciplined well in this age, they will be disciplined in the coming age. Hence, there are four things here that must be distinguished one from the other. The four things, the false Christians, the chastisement in this age, the losing of the kingdom, and the punishment in the millennium, are different from eternal life and death.

Let us now consider the first group, the false Christians. Second Peter 2:1 says, "But there arose also false prophets among the people, as also among you there will be false teachers, who will secretly bring in destructive heresies, even denying the Master who bought them, bringing upon themselves swift destruction." Some would ask if this verse indicates that a Christian can perish. The ones mentioned here are those that have been bought by the Lord. Some will say that this verse obviously says that a Christian can perish, because it says here that they have followed the heresies and have denied the Master who bought them, and their end is swift destruction.

But please remember a few things. Here it mentions the Master who bought them. The word *bought* is used in a particular way. Does the word convey the sense that the bought ones are the saved ones? If these bought ones are the saved ones, then we have to admit that a saved person can perish. But if this word has a different meaning, then one cannot say this any longer. It is true that the Bible tells us that we are bought by the Lord with a price. But we have to see the scope of what the Lord Jesus bought on the cross. Did He buy the believers only, or did He buy the whole world? From the Bible we can see that the Lord did not buy the believers only, but He bought the whole world as well. Matthew 13:44 says, "The kingdom of the heavens is like a treasure hidden in the field, which a man found and hid, and in his joy goes and sells all that he has, and buys that field." This shows us that the Lord Jesus sold whatever He had to buy the treasure. But not only did He buy the treasure, He bought the field as well. The treasure is a small part, but the field is a big part. The treasure is in the field. In order to obtain the treasure, the Lord bought the whole field. The purpose of buying the field was not for the field, but for the treasure. Please remember that the purpose of the Lord's buying was for the small part, but He bought the big part. His purpose is to get the treasure, but the scope of His buying was the field. Those in the kingdom of the heavens are the treasure. But what the Lord bought was the field.

Hence, we cannot say that everyone that is bought by the Lord is saved. The scope of buying is greater than the scope of salvation. The work of buying and redemption on His cross is different from His work of substitution. The Lord's substitution is only for all the believers, but He died for the whole world. He made the scope wide enough. But this does not mean that the whole world is saved. If Peter were to change a word here, if he were to say "denying the Master

370 THE GOSPEL OF GOD

who *saved* them," then it would be very serious. But Peter has used a big enough word. He said "denying the Master who *bought* them." Hence, we can see that this group of people has not been saved at all. This word *bought* is a very broad word. By this word alone, one cannot say that they are saved.

Second, the word Master, *despotes,* here is not a common word either. It should not be translated as lord, but should be translated as master. It is not the Lord as in the Lord Jesus, but the Master as one who has temporal control of a person. It refers to an earthly master. There is no life relationship here. According to a strict interpretation of the Bible, this is not a relationship between them and the Lord, but a relationship between them and their master. Hence, this group of people has not been saved at all. No one can say, Jesus is Lord, except in the Holy Spirit, for whoever calls upon the name of the Lord shall be saved. These ones are like Judas. They have never confessed Jesus as Lord.

Third, Peter tells us that this group of people are the false teachers and the false believers. Peter also told us that there were false prophets among the people. He also said that there will be false teachers. These false prophets refer to the false prophets in the Old Testament. All the readers of the Bible know that no false prophet in the Old Testament was saved. We can say boldly that this group of people have not been saved at all. They followed their cleverness and their ideas, secretly bringing in destructive heresies, and even denying the Master who bought them, bringing upon themselves swift destruction. Hence, 2 Peter 2:1 does not refer to the perdition of the saved ones.

There are more words in the Bible like these. All of them refer to the nominal believers. They do not refer to the perdition of the saved ones. Some have argued about a few words at the end of chapter two. Verse 20 says, "For if, having escaped the defilements of the world by the knowledge of our Lord and Savior Jesus Christ but having again been entangled in these, they are defeated, the last state has become worse for them than the first." Verse 22 says, "It has happened to them according to the true proverb: 'The dog has turned to

its own vomit, and the washed sow to wallowing in the mud.'"
Based on the words of verse 20, some have thought that these
ones refer to the saved ones, because it says plainly that these
ones have escaped the defilements of the world by the
knowledge of our Lord and Savior Jesus Christ; surely such
ones were saved.

But please note that Peter was very careful in the way
he spoke. Verse 20 says that these ones have the knowledge
of our Lord and Savior Jesus Christ, and that they have
escaped the defilements of the world. But verse 22 tells us
who these people really are. If there were only verse 20, we
might think that these are the saved ones. But if we read
verse 22, we will know who they are. "It has happened to
them according to the true proverb: 'The dog has turned to its
own vomit, and the washed sow to wallowing in the mud.'"
It says that although these ones have escaped the defilements
of the world, and outwardly they have the knowledge of our
Lord and Savior Jesus Christ, they were later entangled
again, and their last state has become worse. These people
are simply dogs and sows.

The Lord Jesus has never said that He gives to His dogs
eternal life. Nor has He ever said that His dogs will never
perish. The Lord said that He gives eternal life to the sheep.
He never mixes the sheep with the dogs. He cannot say that
He gives eternal life to the sows and the dogs, nor can He say
that the sheep have been entangled by the defilements of the
world. These two kinds of people can never be mixed together.
Many who have heard the gospel would say that Jesus is Lord
and Savior. They can quickly tell you about doctrines related
to the Lord. Outwardly they do not have any defilements. But
actually they have never been regenerated. They have never
received the Lord and have never experienced the Lord living
in them. They only confess the Lord temporarily. They have
removed a little of the outward defilements. But when
sentiments change, they go back to their old ways. The last
state of this kind of people is worse than their first state.
These are not the sheep at all. They are the dogs and the
sows. Because they are the dogs, they turn to their own vomit.
Because they are the sows, they wallow in the mud after they

have been cleansed without. This does not mean that Christians will not sin, and it does not mean that they will not touch the mud or wallow in the mud. A Christian may touch the mud; he may wallow in the mud. But for a Christian to wallow in the mud is an uncomfortable thing. If he is comfortable in wallowing in it, then he has to be a sow. A Christian could perhaps also swallow his own vomit. But he will feel that it is repulsive, and he will be uncomfortable if he does that. This is the difference between the sow, the dog, and the sheep. One has to identify clearly the nature of the dog and the sow. In the Bible, sows and dogs refer to the unsaved ones. They do not refer to the saved ones. If a person is a sheep, he will never perish.

CHAPTER NINETEEN

SALVATION BEING ETERNAL—
ARGUMENTS AGAINST IT

(3)

In this message we will continue to look at the verses which seem to argue against salvation being eternal.

THE ARGUMENT BASED ON 2 CORINTHIANS 2:7

Second Corinthians 2:6-7 says, "Sufficient for such a one is this punishment by the majority, so that on the contrary you should rather forgive and comfort him, lest perhaps such a one be swallowed up with excessive sorrow." In some translations, the words "swallowed up" are translated as "perish." A brother in Corinth had received punishment by the majority because of his sin. Paul was concerned that the brothers and sisters had dealt with him too severely. He asked them to forgive and encourage such a one, lest he should "perish" with excessive sorrow. Some may argue that if excessive sorrow can cause such a one to perish, is this not an indication that a believer can still perish?

We must realize that this brother is the same one that is mentioned in 1 Corinthians 5. This one committed a gross sin, the sin of fornication of an abnormal sort. Paul said that such a one needs to be removed (vv. 2, 13). The saints in Corinth took Paul's word and removed him. After being removed, he realized that he was sinful, and was in much sorrow and agony over his sin. Paul told the saints in his second Epistle that they had to comfort and encourage him, lest he be swallowed up with excessive sorrow. If we are careless, we may think that "perish" here means to go to hell.

374 of THE GOSPEL OF GOD

Yet Paul in 1 Corinthians 5:5 says "to deliver such a one to Satan for the destruction of his flesh, that his spirit may be saved in the day of the Lord." Based on this word, we can say boldly that such a one was saved. What is mentioned in 2 Corinthians 2:7 is definitely not a matter of the perishing of the spirit.

Second, the word for "be swallowed up" is not a commonly used word. It is a special word in Greek. The word *katapino* denotes something being swallowed up, as a ship sinking in the sea and being swallowed up by it. After such a brother sinned and was excommunicated, he repented. He thought that he was excommunicated and fully rejected. He thought that he had lost all hope. Therefore, he continued in his sorrow and agony. Paul's thought is that if the church would not forgive and comfort him right away, he would be swallowed up by sorrow. This is not a matter of the saving or the perishing of the soul.

THE ARGUMENT BASED ON 2 PETER 3:16

Let us look at another passage. Second Peter 3:16 says, "As also in all his letters, speaking in them concerning these things, in which some things are hard to understand, which the unlearned and unstable twist, as also the rest of the Scriptures, to their own destruction." Some would argue after reading this word that Peter is telling us that Paul's letters were hard to understand, and that some who are unlearned and unstable, that is, untaught and unestablished, bring in their own destruction by twisting Paul's letters. If they can be destroyed, does this not indicate that they will perish? Will a saved person perish? In this case Peter is not talking about eternal perdition at all.

According to the Bible, whether one perishes or not does not depend on the way that he interprets the Scripture. Today in China, I have seen a number of good Christians who love the Lord and who labor everywhere in the gospel work. Yet they do not really understand Paul's letters. When they preach, they do more than twist the word of the Scriptures. Are these Christians going to perish? Can a wrong exposition of the Scriptures be a factor of perdition? The Bible never makes a sound exposition of the Bible a condition for salvation. Hence, Peter's word here must mean something else.

Second, the word *apoleia* in Greek does not refer to an ordinary kind of destruction. It is different from the one used in 2 Corinthians 2:7. It is different from the usual word for "perdition." In Greek, this word, *apollyon*, means to destroy or to be corrupted. If something is taken from you smoothly, it is a "taking"; if something is wrung out of your hands by force, it is an *apollyon*. What Peter meant in his Epistle is that some misunderstood Paul's letters and did not have light from God. They twisted his word in the same way that something is wrung out of a person's hand. In so doing, they were destroying themselves and not building up themselves. Destruction is the opposite of building. If you are not being built up, you are being destroyed. By so doing, you will not be built up but will have your work destroyed. Hence, these two verses do not tell us that a man can perish after being saved. They tell us of those whose work and living after salvation are not perfected, and who are unable to be built up day by day. If you twist Paul's Epistles, you are destroying what you already have.

THE ARGUMENT BASED ON HEBREWS 10:26

There is another portion of Scripture that we must mention. It is also a passage that many do not understand. Hebrews 10:26-29 says, "For when we sin willfully after receiving the knowledge of the truth, there no longer remains a sacrifice of bulls and goats for sins, but a certain fearful expectation of judgment and fervor of fire, which is to consume the adversaries. Anyone who has set aside the law of Moses dies without compassion on the testimony of two or three witnesses. By how much do you think he will be thought worthy of worse punishment who has trampled underfoot the Son of God and has considered the blood of the covenant by which he was sanctified a common thing and has insulted the Spirit of grace?" The person mentioned in this portion of the Word must be saved, because he has already had the sacrifice for sins. The apostle said that if one who already had the sacrifice for sins sinned willfully, there would be no more sacrifice for sins. We have no problem after verse 27. However, the verse that many readers of the Bible find difficult to understand is verse 26, which says, "There no longer remains a sacrifice of bulls and goats for sins." Some people think that if, unfortunately, a Christian commits sins willfully, there will be no more sacrifice for sins for him. In this case, it would mean that he will surely perish. Hebrews 10:26 is a problem to many people. When I was first saved, I also thought that this verse was a big problem. For over a year, I considered myself unsaved because of this verse. For this reason, we have to spend an amount of time to find out what Hebrews 10:26 speaks of.

The first thing that we need to mention is the word "willfully." What is meant by "willfully"? Does this word mean "consciously"? This may be the answer that we would give. But I would ask if there are many Christians who sin unconsciously? Every day we sin. Yet how many times do we sin unconsciously? I believe that probably every time we sin, we sin "willfully." Very few people commit sins unconsciously. Most of the time, we sin "willfully." In Romans 7, Paul says, "For what I work out, I do not acknowledge; for what I will, this I do not practice; but what I hate, this I do" (v. 15). By this we know that Paul did not fall into sin accidentally. All of his sins were committed after he was fully conscious of their wrong. Hence, it is clear from Romans 7 that all of Paul's sins were committed "willfully." If Paul sinned "willfully," then according to Hebrews 10:26, there would remain no longer any sacrifice for sins. If a person perished and went to hell, he would see Paul there, because even Paul had no more sacrifice for sins. Hence, we need to see that the word "willfully" in Hebrews 10:26 does not mean consciously. If this were the case, then all of the Christians would perish. No matter what kind of Christian you may be, countless times in your life, you sin consciously rather than unconsciously. If the above situation were true, no Christian would be saved. Hence, "willfully" here must mean something else.

A second point is that verse 26 begins with the word "for." For this particular word to be used at the beginning of a sentence, something has gone on prior to its use. This word cannot be used without a preceding sentence. In verses 26 through 29, the first sentence begins with "for," which means that there was something mentioned before. Prior to this, verse 25 says, "Not abandoning our own assembling together, as the custom with some is, but exhorting one another; and so much the more as you see the day drawing near." Why should we not abandon our own assembling together, but exhort one another? It is because when we sin willfully after receiving the full knowledge of the truth, there no longer remains a sacrifice for sins. If we do not read this portion carefully, we will not realize that these two verses go together. If we read it carefully, we will realize that these two verses are linked together. They are very meaningful. We must realize that *not abandoning our own assembling together* and *sinning willfully* go together. We must not forsake the assembling of ourselves together, but exhort one another, for when we sin willfully, there no longer remains a sacrifice for sins. Negatively, we should not forsake the assembling of ourselves together. Positively, we must not sin willfully. If we assemble ourselves together, then we are not ones who sin willfully. If we customarily forsake the assembling of ourselves together, we are ones who sin willfully. Here, the apostle put the abandoning of our assembling and sinning willfully together. Why is there such a close relationship between abandoning the assembling of ourselves and sinning willfully? At this juncture we must come to the third point. We have to know the background of the book of Hebrews. Who were the ones mentioned in this book? They were the Jews who believed in the Lord Jesus. Hence, the book of Hebrews was written to believing Jews. The position of the Jews is different from that of the Gentiles. The Gentiles have the spiritual position only and not the earthly, physical position. The Jews have both a spiritual and a physical position. They have a heavenly as well as an earthly position. Today when we speak of the Holy of Holies, immediately we think of a place where God dwells in heaven. But to the Jews, when they consider the Holy of Holies, what occurs in their thought is the Holy of Holies inside the temple at Jerusalem on Mount Moriah. Not only do the Jews have a Holy of Holies in heaven, but they also have a Holy of Holies on the earth. Not only do they have a temple in heaven, but a temple on earth also. Thus, in their mind, there is the spiritual aspect as well as the physical aspect, the heavenly aspect as well as the earthly. They have the Old Testament as well as the New Testament. They still have the physical Holy of Holies, and with it the offerings.

To us, the sacrifice for sins is the Lord Jesus Christ; He is our sin offering. Yet, the Jews were still not clear whether the Lord Jesus Christ or bulls and goats was their sacrifice for sins. At that time, they still had the priests, the altar, and the sacrifices of bulls and goats on the altar. Not only did they have the spiritual sacrifice for sins, they also had the earthly sacrifices for sins. Christians and Jews do not stand on the same ground. The Gentile believers are different from the Hebrew believers. In A.D. 70 the Roman prince Titus destroyed the temple at Jerusalem, and not one stone was left upon another. However, when the book of Hebrews was written, the earthly temple was still there, and the sacrifices were still being offered. After a number of Jews had believed in the Lord Jesus, they had to make a decision whether they wanted the earthly altar or the heavenly one, the earthly sacrifices or the heavenly sacrifice. At that time, the Jews could not have both the heavenly and the earthly sacrifices at the same time. Everyone who reads the book of Hebrews knows that this book was written with the purpose that Christians would forsake Judaism and would accept Christianity. The purpose of the book of Hebrews is to encourage the Christians to drop the earthly sacrifices and to accept the heavenly sacrifice. This is the background of the book.

Therefore, when it says that one should not abandon the assembling of oneself together, it does not mean that the assembling of Christians can save them or qualify them to have eternal life. The assembling of Christians indicates whether a believer wants Judaism or Christ. The assembling of ourselves becomes an expression of our attitude toward Christ. At that time, all those who assembled together were Christians. No matter if you were a Gentile or a Jew, if you assembled together, you were a Christian. Hence, assembling together became a sign of accepting Christ, and forsaking the assembling together was a sign of forsaking Christ to embrace Judaism. In the same way, sinning willfully here does not refer to things such as murder, arson, eating, drinking, gambling, and licentiousness. Sinning willfully here does not refer to moral sins; it refers to doctrinal sins. This does not pertain to whether or not your walk is proper. This refers to the fact of whether or not you receive Christ or Judaism. To assemble yourselves together means that you want Christ and that you stand on the ground of Christ. To abandon the assembling together shows that you have your back toward Christ and that your face is toward Judaism. To abandon the assembling means that you want the earthly temple, the earthly altar, and the earthly sacrifices. This indicates that you want to go back to Judaism and forsake Christ. If this is the fact, there no longer remains a sacrifice for sins.

Now let us return to the first point. Verse 26 says, "After receiving the knowledge of the truth." It does not say, "After being regenerated," nor does it say, "After our sinful deeds are washed away." If it had said, "After being regenerated" or "After being washed," then to sin willfully would be a matter of our conduct. However, it says, "After receiving the knowledge of the truth"; it is a matter of knowing. Do we know what the truth is? The truth is the faith of a Christian. The truth is that God sent His Son into the world that He would become the sin offering. The truth is that God sent His Son to die for us and resurrect to satisfy all of God's requirements. All of these have to do with the items of faith on God's side. Hence, to sin willfully does not mean transgressions in life. It means to sin against the truth. This is not a behavioral sin, but a doctrinal sin, and a sin regarding one's belief. This is a sin that opposes the faith and the truth, after receiving the full knowledge of the truth.

The Hebrew believers were Jews and had been in Judaism for years. Now that they were Christians, if they still wanted to go back to Judaism, if they still wanted both, that is, if they wanted to stand on the ground of Judaism and also wanted to stand on the ground of Christianity, there would no longer remain a sacrifice for sins. In ancient times, the Chinese worshipped idols. The Temple of Heaven in Beijing was the place where emperors offered sacrifices. There men killed bulls and offered them to the highest deity in heaven. It was the earthly emperor offering up sacrifices to the highest deity in heaven in order to redeem the sins of the people. Suppose the earthly emperor believed in the Lord Jesus. Do you think that he could go back to the Temple of Heaven to offer sacrifices? After he received Christ as the sacrifice for sin, he could not go back to the Temple of Heaven to offer sacrifices anymore. Either he took the Temple of Heaven or the Lord Jesus. This is what the Bible means by sinning willfully. This is not a matter of sin in our conduct.

Verse 26 continues, "There no longer remains a sacrifice of bulls and goats for sins." The words "no longer" mean "again." Whenever the words "no longer" appear, this shows that there must be something in the foregoing verses. Some misunderstand the Word of God. They think that the sentence, "There no longer remains a sacrifice of bulls and goats for sins" implies perdition. This is absolutely not God's thought.

We have to look at Hebrews 7:27b, which says, "For this He did once for all when He offered up Himself." This tells us that after the Lord Jesus offered up Himself once before God as the sacrifice for sins, everything was fully accomplished. Please take heed to the word "once." Let us take a look at Hebrews 9:12b, which says, "Entered once for all into the Holy of Holies, obtaining an eternal redemption." Here it tells us again that the Lord Jesus offered Himself only once, and then the work of redemption was eternally accomplished. Let us look at the word "once" again. Hebrews 9:25-28 says, "Nor in order that He might offer Himself often, just as the high priest enters into the Holy of Holies year by year by the blood of other creatures; since then He would have had to suffer often since the foundation of the world. But now once at the consummation of the ages He has been manifested for the putting away of sin through the sacrifice of Himself. And inasmuch as it is reserved for men to die once, and after this comes judgment, so Christ also, having been offered once to bear the sins of many, will appear a second time to those who eagerly await Him, apart from sin, unto salvation." Twice these verses mention "often," and twice the word "once" is used in reference to Christ. Not often, but once for all, Christ offered Himself up before God as the sacrifice for sins and completed the work of redemption. Please take heed to the word "often" and the word "once" here.

Hebrews 10:10 says, "By which will we have been sanctified through the offering of the body of Jesus Christ once for all." Verse 12 says, "But this One, having offered one sacrifice for sins, sat down forever on the right hand of God." Verse 14 continues, "For by one offering He has perfected forever those who are being sanctified." The earthly priests had to offer sacrifices to God time after time. Yet, Christ offered Himself only once, and we are sanctified. After Christ offered Himself once as the eternal sacrifice, He sat down on the right hand of God. He sat down because He does not have to work anymore. He offered Himself once, and we are eternally perfected. Since He has already completed His work, there is no problem anymore.

Therefore, after reading so many verses, we can know the meaning of the verse, "There no longer remains a sacrifice of bulls and goats for sins." The portion of Hebrews from chapters seven through ten, with the exception of chapter eight, says that the work of redemption, once finished, is eternally accomplished. If you do not want Christ, there no longer remains a sacrifice for sins. Christ only offered Himself once as the sacrifice for sins. If you do not want the redemption of Christ, but turn to Judaism, you will no longer find any other sacrifice for sins. So, it is not a matter of being saved or perishing here. What is said here is that the work of Christ is accomplished once. If you do not want this sacrifice, you will no longer have a second one.

If you take heed to the words "no longer," you will see what they are linked to. The foregoing verses repeatedly mention the words "once for all," and the following verse says, "There no longer remains." It is equivalent to saying, for example, in chapter eight, "Here is the only pencil." Then in chapter nine I repeat, "Here is the only pencil." Again in chapter ten I say, "Here is the only pencil." After this I may explain, "If you do not want this pencil, or if you want to exchange this for another one, there will not be another one. Take this one if you want it. If you do not want it, there is no other one left for you." This verse does not mean that after receiving the knowledge of the truth, and then sinning willfully, you will not receive forgiveness anymore. This is not a matter of sin. This is a matter of the truth, a matter of the Christian faith. If you forsake the Christian faith and look for another Savior, another sacrifice for sins, you will not find it.

Some of the Jews at that time probably thought that if they rejected the Christian faith, they could still go back to the temple. They could still go back to the altar and have the priests offer bulls and goats for them. But this would indicate another sacrifice for sins. The Jews during that time still had the priests and the altar. Their believing in Christ was different from our believing in Christ. To them, they could choose to believe or not to believe. They were not like the Gentile believers, who could only go back to idol worship if they did not believe. If the Gentile believers wanted God, they could choose God. But if they did not want God, their only choice would be the world. They did not have a third choice. With the Jews, it was different. The Jews thought that if they did not want Christ, they could still be saved. If they did not want Christ, they could still have redemption for sins, because they still could keep the priests and the offerings. If they had more money, they could buy a bull. If they did not have that much money, they could still purchase a goat.

The apostle was telling the Jews that Christ had already offered Himself once for all and had completed the eternal redemptive work before God. God had already abolished the old covenant together with the old sacrifices. Before the coming of Christ, the bulls and goats could atone for their sins. But after the coming of Christ, the sacrifices of the bulls and goats could no longer take away their sins; these sacrifices have actually been abolished. This is what Hebrews chapters seven through ten point out. God not only gave His

Son as the sacrifice, but He abolished the sacrifices of bulls and goats. The first half of chapter ten mentions that God does not take pleasure in bulls and goats, nor does He take pleasure in burnt offerings and sacrifices for sins. God prepared His Son. Bulls and goats cannot redeem men from their sins. Only His Son can redeem us from sins. The sacrifice of bulls and goats in the Old Testament were only types and shadows. They refer to the Son of God as *the* sacrifice. God said that the old covenant is a thing of the past; the types are over, and the reality is here. It will no longer be acceptable if they reject God's Son, that is, if they reject the reality and offer up the types. According to God, there is only one sacrifice for sins. Besides Him, there is no other sacrifice for sins. Hebrews 10:26 tells us that if we forsake Christ to look for another Savior, we will not find one.

Hence, strictly speaking, this portion is not for us at all. If some say that after a man receives the Lord Jesus and sins willfully, he will perish, this will contradict the context of the passage; it will also contradict the entire book of Hebrews. The speaking here is about a doctrinal issue. Hebrews shows us that besides the name of Jesus Christ, "there is salvation in no other, for neither is there another name under heaven given among men in which we must be saved" (Acts 4:12). This does not mean that a Christian will go to hell if he sins.

Hebrews 10:27 says, "But a certain fearful expectation of judgment and fervor of fire, which is to consume the adversaries." After receiving the knowledge of the truth, and after having a clear knowledge that the Lord Jesus Christ is the God-ordained sacrifice for sins, if the Jewish believers forsake the assembling of themselves and reject Christ, and if they go back to Judaism to look for other sacrifices for sins, there will no longer remain any sacrifice for sins. They can only expect judgment in fear and the fervor of fire that consumes the adversaries. Before they were saved, they could depend on bulls and goats to atone for their sins. But after they realize that the Lord Jesus is the only Savior, they cannot depend on bulls and goats anymore. If they reject the Lord

Jesus, they can only expect a fearful judgment and fervor of fire about to consume the adversaries. They can only take the Lord Jesus as the Savior. Besides Him, there is no other way of salvation. All of the bulls and goats point to Christ. Bulls and goats are but types of Christ. Christ is the reality of the bulls and goats. It is impossible for them to reject the reality of the bulls and goats and ask for the types instead. Hence, Hebrews 10:26-27 never says that after a person is saved he may still perish. This is man's twisting of God's truth.

When we read the Bible, we have to read what is there instead of reading into it what is not there. Someone asked me once how he could understand the Bible. I answered that to understand the Bible, we must first be those who do not understand the Bible. If we do not understand, then we will understand. If we say that we know this and that, then we are not sober-minded. Once we are not sober-minded, we will have problems. Hebrews 6 and 10 should be as easy and simple and clear as John 3:16. The reason the human mind is unclear is that man puts his own words into the Bible. Many people find it difficult to read the Bible, not because the Bible is unclear, but because in their minds they have prejudices and preconceived ideas.

CHAPTER TWENTY

HOW GOD DEALS
WITH THE BELIEVERS' SINS—
DISCIPLINE AND REWARD

We have to differentiate two things in the Bible: God's discipline of believers in this age and their salvation in eternity. In the previous message, we saw the first difference. In this message, we are going to see the second. Hebrews records the matter of the discipline of the believers. Now we have to see what are the kinds of people that God disciplines and what is the purpose of this discipline.

THE MOTIVE AND GOAL OF DISCIPLINE

Hebrews 12:5-6 says, "And you have completely forgotten the exhortation which reasons with you as with sons, 'My son, do not regard lightly the discipline of the Lord, nor faint when reproved by Him; for whom the Lord loves He disciplines, and He scourges every son whom He receives.'" Here, we see clearly that the motive of discipline is the love of God. Those who receive God's discipline are the sons of God. If someone is not a son of God, God will not discipline him. You can never find in the Bible that God disciplines an unbeliever. God does not waste His time and energy to discipline all the people on this earth. It is the same with us. We do not discipline our neighbors' children. If the neighbors' children do not dress well or do things properly, we do not discipline them. Only when it is a case of our own children do we discipline them. Therefore, the realm of discipline is confined only to Christians, and the motive of discipline is love. It is not because God hates man that He disciplines him. He disciplines man because He loves him. Revelation 3:19 also says that God disciplines because of love.

Hebrews 12:7-8 says, "It is for discipline that you endure; God deals with you as with sons. For what son is there whom the father does not discipline? But if you are without discipline, of which all sons have become partakers, then you are illegitimate and not sons." Therefore, the extent of discipline is limited to the children only. Verse 9 says, "Furthermore we have had the fathers of our flesh as discipliners and we respected them; shall we not much more be in subjection to the Father of spirits and live?" If we accept the discipline of our parents in the flesh, how much more should we accept the discipline from our Father, the Father of spirits.

Verse 10 says, "For they disciplined for a few days as it seemed good to them; but He, for what is profitable that we might partake of His holiness." This tells us the purpose of discipline. It is not because God likes to discipline us that He does it. Neither is it because He wants us to suffer. He disciplines us so that we can partake of His holiness. If a Christian lives in a very loose way on earth, without manifesting God's nature and holiness, God's hand will fall heavily on such a one. God does not like to chastise us. His purpose is to have His holiness manifested in us. He will only stop disciplining us when His holiness is manifested in us. Therefore, we see that discipline does not prove that we are not the Lord's. Rather, it proves that we belong to the Lord. There is no need of discipline for someone who does not belong to the Lord. Only those who belong to the Lord are qualified to be disciplined.

There is a big difference between punishment and discipline. God's disciplining of His children is not His punishment upon them. Even when God chastises them, this chastisement is not a punishment, but a discipline. Discipline is with a definite goal, which is that we may partake of His holiness, that we may not live foolishly day by day. After a Christian believes into the Lord Jesus, although he will never lose his salvation, he may receive severe chastisement from God. We should never say that a Christian can do whatever he wants after he is saved. The Bible clearly tells us that after a Christian is saved, even if he is defeated and fallen, he will not perish eternally and will not lose eternal life. However, he will receive God's chastising on earth today.

We should not make the mistake of thinking that because we are eternally saved, we can live loosely on this earth. No one can refute the fact that once a person is saved, he is eternally saved. This is a fact. If a Christian unbridles his lusts, commits sins, falls into defilements, and does not have God's holiness, God will extend His hand and will discipline such a one through his environment, his family, his personal health, and his future plans. He may encounter difficulties in his family. He may experience much illness and misfortune in his environment. The purpose of God in allowing these things to fall upon him is not a matter of punishing him; they are not there to give him a hard time, but to make him partake of God's holiness and to become worthy of the grace of His calling. This is the proper understanding of salvation.

One should not say that if a Christian does not do good, God will deny that he is a child of God and kick him out like a dog. If one would say such a thing, either he is blind to the work of the cross of Christ, or he thinks that the work of Christ is a very light matter.

The Bible shows us that salvation is eternal. At the same time, the Bible also shows us that there are quite serious punishments among the believers. If we fail, there will be much punishment for us. God wants us to partake of His holiness. On this earth He wants us to live like sons of God. He does not want to intimidate us with hell so that we will pursue holiness. To be saved is totally of grace, but God has His way to lead us into His holiness. He causes us to encounter many things in our families, in our bodies, in our career, and in our environment so that we will turn back to Him. This is the purpose of discipline.

Ananias and Sapphira were believers; they were saved. They committed the sin of lying to the Spirit, and they received a very severe discipline (Acts 5:1-10). At one time, I thought that perhaps Ananias and Sapphira were not saved. By reading the Bible carefully, one has to acknowledge that they were saved because they were with the disciples at the time of Pentecost. In addition, they also made an offering. They were only after some vain glory. Their sins were not as severe as one would think. They did not get drunk or commit fornication. The fact that they were taken from the world quickly proves that they were believers. If they were worldly people, they probably would have lived much longer. The fact that they were removed quickly from the world proves that they were our brother and sister.

The Corinthian believers did not respect the Lord's table meeting. They did not respect the Body of the Lord, and they treated the Lord's supper loosely. What were the results of these things? Paul says in 1 Corinthians 11:29-30, "He who eats and drinks, eats and drinks judgment to himself if he does not discern the body. Because of this many among you are weak and sick, and a number sleep." The disciplining hand of God makes people sick and weak and even causes them to die. God treated them this way because they treated the Body of the Lord lightly. They did not see the Lord's death nor the work of Christ, and they did not see the Body of Christ. They did not see the respect they should render to the Lord Jesus, and they did not see their proper standing in the Body of Christ. This resulted in weakness, in sickness, and even in death. After they had sinned, God disciplined them.

Verse 32 says, "But being judged by the Lord, we are disciplined that we may not be condemned with the world." There is a purpose in God's discipline. It is to save us from condemnation in the future. God disciplines us so that we will not fall into the condemnation that the world will receive. In other words, discipline proves that we are saved. Discipline preserves our salvation. God's way and our way of doing things are totally different. We think that if we tell people that they are saved, they will be loose and unrestrained. God is not like this. He proclaims clearly, absolutely, and without limitation to all those who believe in Him that all who believe have eternal life and will not perish. But He has His way of saving us from sinning and keeping us from being wanton and loose Christians. His discipline is a substitute for our being condemned. Man may think that condemnation is the best method to keep us from sinning, but God does not use the way of condemnation. Rather, He uses the way of discipline. It is very clear that God separates the believers from the worldly people by discipline. The matters of discipline and salvation must be clearly differentiated. Discipline is exercised only for the present and has nothing to do with our eternal salvation.

There is a good example in 1 Corinthians to show that discipline for a Christian proves that he is saved. Even if a Christian has committed a very gross sin, he is still saved. First Corinthians 5 talks about a Christian who committed adultery. Such an act of adultery with one's stepmother was not even found among the unbelievers. Those who are clear about the law of Moses would say that this person will surely perish and is guaranteed to go to hell. But surprisingly, 1 Corinthians shows us clearly that here is one who had committed a very grave and despicable sin; it is a sin that is not committed by ordinary people. Paul says that with the power of the Lord Jesus, he delivered such a one to Satan for the destruction of the flesh, that is to allow Satan to exhibit his power on the body of this one to cause him to be weak, to be ill, and even to die. The purpose of Paul in doing this was that this one may be saved in the day of the Lord. Discipline is something for this life. It is absolutely not related to salvation in eternity. If it were up to us, we would say, "It is finished. Although such a one has been saved, surely he will perish again because of committing such a gross sin." However, Paul says that this one will not perish even though he has committed such a sin. A saved one can temporarily receive discipline, but he cannot be penalized with eternal perdition. This is the teaching of Paul. A Christian can have temporary discipline in this age, but he cannot perish eternally. We may need discipline, but we will still be saved in eternity. Paul made a clear distinction between these two things many times in the New Testament. The destruction mentioned here and the sleep mentioned before relate to the body only; they do not refer to the spirit. The matters of the

spirit and of eternal salvation were decided already when we
believed in the Lord.

Some people have a problem with 1 John 5:16, where it
says that we should not make request for anyone who has
committed a sin unto death. They have this problem because
they do not understand the Word of God. They think that to
sin unto death as spoken of here means perdition. Actually
there is no such thing. First John 5:16 tells us of some people
who sinned to the extent that God would have them die and
their flesh removed from the world. The death mentioned in
1 Corinthians 11, the destruction in 1 Corinthians 5, and the
deaths of Ananias and Sapphira are all deaths of the flesh
and have nothing to do with the death of the spirit. Discipline
is totally a matter with the body. Therefore, in the Bible,
many places which seem to say that believers may perish are
actually speaking about discipline.

REWARD AND GIFT

Now we want to see the third difference—the difference
between reward and gift, in other words, the difference
between the kingdom and eternal life. There are many
Christians in the church today who cannot differentiate
between the kingdom of the heavens and eternal life. They
think that the kingdom of the heavens is eternal life and
that eternal life is simply the kingdom of the heavens. They
have mixed up the Word of God, taking the condition for the
receiving of the kingdom as the condition for the preservation
of eternal life. They take the losing of the kingdom as the
losing of eternal life. However, the distinction between these
two is very clear in the Bible. One may lose the kingdom of
the heavens, but he will not lose eternal life. One can lose
the reward, but he will not lose the gift.

What then is the reward, and what is the gift? We were
saved because of the gift. God gave the gift to us freely by
His grace; therefore, we were saved. The reward pertains to
the relationship between us and the Holy Spirit after we were
saved. When we were saved, we were related to Christ. This
relationship allows us to obtain the gift that we are absolutely
unworthy of receiving. Similarly, after we have been saved,

we have a relationship with the Holy Spirit. This relationship allows us to obtain the reward which we could not otherwise obtain by ourselves. If one believes in the Lord Jesus as Savior, accepting the Lord Jesus as life, this one is saved before God. After he is saved, God immediately puts this one on a pathway, so that he will run in the race and will obtain the reward placed before him. A Christian is saved because of the Lord Jesus. After he is saved, he has to manifest the victory of Christ by the Holy Spirit day by day. If one will do this, then at the end of the race, he will obtain the heavenly glory and the heavenly reward from God.

Hence, salvation is the first step of this path, and the reward is the last step. Only the saved ones are qualified to gain the reward. The unsaved ones are not qualified for this. God has given us two things rather than one thing. God places the gift before the worldly people and places the reward before the Christians. When one believes in Christ, he receives the gift. When one follows Christ, he receives the reward. Gift is obtained through faith, and it is for the worldly people. Reward is obtained by being faithful and having good deeds, and it is for the Christians.

There is a big mistake in the churches today. Man thinks that salvation is the only thing and that there is nothing else besides being saved. He takes the kingdom of the heavens and eternal life as the same thing. He considers that since one is saved when he believes, he no longer has to be concerned with works. The Bible makes a distinction between God's part and man's part. One part is the salvation given by God, and the other part is the glory of the millennial kingdom. To be saved has absolutely nothing to do with one's works. Once anyone believes in the Lord Jesus, he is saved. But after his salvation, God immediately places the second thing before him, telling him that besides salvation, there is a reward, a coming glory, a crown, and a throne for him. God puts His throne, crown, glory, and reward before the believers. If one is faithful, he will obtain these. If he is unfaithful, he will lose them.

Therefore, we do not say that good works are useless. However, we do say that good works are useless as far as

salvation is concerned. Man cannot be saved by his good
works. Neither can he be prevented from salvation by his evil
works. Good works are applicable to the matter of the reward,
the matter of the crown, the matter of the glory, and the
matter of the throne. Good works are useless regarding
the matter of salvation. God cannot allow man to be saved
by his work; neither will He allow man to be rewarded by
his faith. God cannot allow man to perish because of his evil
works. God can determine only man's salvation or perdition
by whether or not he believes in His Son. Similarly, God
cannot determine a man's receiving of His glory by whether
or not one believes in His Son. Whether or not you have His
Son in you determines the matter of eternal life or perdition.
Whether or not you have good works before God determines
the matter of receiving the reward and the glory. In other
words, God will never save a person because he has merits,
and He will never reward one who has no merit. If someone
has merits, God will not therefore save such a one. On the
other hand, God will never reward anyone who has no merit.
Man has to come before God totally helpless and meritless
in order for God to save him. But after salvation, we have to
be faithful, and we have to endeavor to produce good works
through His Son Jesus Christ in order to obtain the reward.

Please do not think that good works are useless. We are
saying that good works are useless towards salvation. Good
works have nothing to do with salvation at all. Salvation
depends on whether or not you would repent of your former
position. It depends on whether you would have regret over
your past to believe in His work on the cross and in His
resurrection as the proof of your justification. This is the
crux of all problems. The matter of work is related to reward.
Work is useful, but only in the matter of reward.

Today's problem is that people will not differentiate
between salvation and the kingdom. In the Bible, there is a
clear distinction between salvation and the kingdom and
between the gift and the reward. Because people would not
differentiate these matters, the question of salvation is
mishandled, and the question of reward is also mishandled.
God has never placed the matter of reward before the unsaved

ones. God only wants the unsaved ones to obtain salvation. However, after salvation, God places the reward before them so that they will endeavor, pursue, and run after the reward. Salvation is not the last step of the Christian experience. Rather, salvation is its first step. After we have been saved, we have to run and pursue after the reward before us. The problem is that we think that our salvation is our reward. The sinners think that to be saved is to obtain the reward, and therefore they rely on their works. The Christians think that the glory is simply grace, and therefore they become foolish in their living. Please apply work only to reward and grace to salvation.

Through salvation God separates the saved ones from the unsaved ones; He separates the ones having eternal life from those being condemned. Similarly, God also separates His children into two groups by His reward. Just as salvation separates the worldly people, in the same way, reward also separates God's children. God separates His children into the obedient and disobedient ones. With the worldly people, it is a matter of having faith and not having faith. With the Christians, it is a matter of being faithful or not being faithful. With the worldly people, it is a question of being saved or not being saved. With the Christians, it is a matter of having or not having the reward. Today's problem with God's children is that they magnify salvation too much; all that they see is simply salvation. They think that only when their work is taken care of can they be saved. As a result, they have no more time to pursue after the reward. If one has not passed through the first gate, he cannot pass through the second. May God be merciful to us that we would realize that the matter of salvation is solved already. It cannot be shaken, for it has been accomplished by the Lord Jesus already. It is fully done. Today what we have to strive for is the reward before us. There will be a big differentiation in the kingdom. Some will have glory, and some will not have glory.

Now we need to see on what basis reward is given. God's Word says that the reward is given because of work. Just as the Bible says clearly that salvation is by faith, in the same

way the Bible says clearly that reward is by work. The Bible
reveals to us that salvation is by the faith of the sinners,
and the reward is by the work of the Christians. Faith is
related to salvation; this is more than clear. Work is related
to reward; this is also more than clear. One should not mix
up these two.

Romans 4:4 says, "Now to the one who works, his wages
are not accounted according to grace, but according to what
is due." To give a reward to one who works is not grace, but
a debt. In other words, how can one obtain a reward? Reward
comes by works and not by grace.

Revelation 2:23 says, "And her children I will kill with
death; and all the churches will know that I am He who
searches the inward parts and the hearts; and I will give to
each one of you according to your works." This verse says
that the Lord will make all the churches know that He is the
One who searches the inward parts and the hearts, and will
give to each one according to his works. In other words, He
will reward each one according to his works. How does He
reward or recompense? It is according to our work. Of course,
this work is not our own work. We only wash our clothes to
be white in the blood. When the Holy Spirit lives out Christ
in us, we have the works of a Christian. Some will live out
Christ, and some will not live out Christ. All the capital comes
from Christ. All the power also originates from Christ. But
some let the Lord work within them and some do not.
Therefore, this verse clearly shows us the matter of recompense. The matter of reward depends on whether or not a
Christian is worthy. Today God will not save a person who
is worthy, and in the future God will not reward a Christian
who is not worthy.

First Corinthians 3:14 says, "If anyone's work which he
has built upon the foundation remains, he will receive a
reward." Here it says that if his work remains, he will be
rewarded. It does not say that if his faith remains he will
be rewarded. The matter of reward depends on one's work.
The Bible distinguishes clearly between salvation and reward.
It never mixes up salvation and reward, and it never mixes
up faith and work. Without faith, man cannot be saved.

Without good works, man cannot be rewarded. One's works must withstand before the judgment seat and survive under the scrutiny of the burning eyes before there is the possibility of receiving a reward.

Luke 6:35 says, "But love your enemies, and do good and lend, expecting nothing in return, and your reward will be great." Reward is entirely due to one's work. To lend money to another without hoping to be repaid is your work, and to love your enemy is your work. You have to do these to obtain the reward. Nowhere does the Bible mention that one has to love his enemies and do good before he can receive eternal life. Neither is there any verse that says one has to lend to others before he can be saved, or that he has to lend to others before he can avoid perdition. But there is such a verse that says if you lend to others and do good to others, your reward in heaven will be great. Reward is of work and not of faith. Faith can save you, but faith cannot help you obtain the reward.

Second Timothy 4:14 says, "Alexander the coppersmith did many evil things to me; the Lord will recompense him according to his works." Here an example is cited. A Christian was trying to hurt Paul; he had sinned against Paul. The person mentioned here was a Christian. He was not a worldly person. In the future, Christians will be rewarded before God according to their works.

THE REWARD BEING THE KINGDOM OF THE HEAVENS

Let us go on. Many people know that there is a difference between salvation and reward. But there are many people who do not see what the reward is. In the Bible, whether with the Lord Jesus, or with the apostles, the words they spoke concerning the reward and the kingdom were not spoken lightly, in the same way the gift and eternal life were not spoken of lightly. When the Lord Jesus says in the Gospel of John that He gives eternal life to His sheep, He is speaking reality and not some empty words (John 10:28). Romans 6 says that the gift of God is eternal life in Christ Jesus our Lord (v. 23). It is so clear that the gift of God is eternal life. What then is the reward? The Bible clearly shows us that the reward is the crown, the throne, and the kingdom of the heavens. The kingdom of the heavens is the reward. In the Bible, there are three aspects to the kingdom of the heavens. In the first aspect, the kingdom of the heavens is theout-ward manifestation of God's authority today; it is the outward manifestation of God's sovereignty. The Bible calls this the kingdom of the heavens. The second aspect is the authority of the heavens controlling and limiting man. This is also called the kingdom of the heavens. However, there is a third aspect of the kingdom of the heavens; it refers to the reward.

The Lord's sermon on the mount in Matthew 5—7 speaks of the kingdom of the heavens. These teachings of the Lord tell us how man can enter into the kingdom of the heavens. Matthew 5—7 repeatedly speaks of the matter of reward. We see very clearly that the words "the kingdom of the heavens" and the word "reward" are found together many times. Many are familiar with the Beatitudes. The Chinese call them the Eight Blessings. Actually, there are nine blessings in the Beatitudes. Blessed are the poor in spirit, for theirs is the kingdom of the heavens. Blessed are those who mourn, for they shall be comforted. Blessed are the meek, for they shall inherit the earth. Blessed are those who hunger and thirst for righteousness, for they shall be satisfied. Blessed are the pure in heart, for they shall see God. Also, blessed are those who are persecuted for the sake of righteousness, for theirs is the kingdom of the heavens. The kingdom of the heavens is mentioned twice in these few blessings. At the end, the Lord says, "Blessed are you when they reproach and persecute you, and while speaking lies, say every evil thing against you because of Me. Rejoice and exult, for your reward is great in the heavens" (Matt. 5:11-12). Here we must admit that the reward is the kingdom of the heavens. The Lord begins by saying that this kind and that kind of people are blessed because the kingdom of the heavens is theirs. At the end He says that these people are blessed because their reward is great in the heavens. These parallel sentences show us that the kingdom of the heavens is God's reward. There is no difference between the two.

In the sermon on the mount, the Lord mentioned the

matter of the reward many times because this portion concerns the kingdom. Matthew 5:46 says, "For if you love those who love you, what reward do you have?" Matthew 6:1-2 says, "But take care not to do your righteousness before men in order to be gazed at by them; otherwise, you have no reward with your Father who is in the heavens. Therefore when you give alms, do not sound a trumpet before you as the hypocrites do in the synagogues and in the streets, so that they may be glorified by men. Truly I say to you, They have their reward in full." Verse 5 says, "And when you pray, you shall not be like the hypocrites....They have their reward in full." Verse 16 says, "And when you fast, do not be like the sullen-faced hypocrites....They have their reward in full." Verse 4 says, "So that your alms may be in secret; and your Father who sees in secret will repay you." Verse 6 says, "But you, when you pray, enter into your private room, and shut your door and pray to your Father who is in secret; and your Father who sees in secret will repay you." The last part of verse 18 says, "And your Father who sees in secret will repay you." Every reader of the Bible agrees that the main subject of the sermon on the mount in Matthew 5—7 is the kingdom of the heavens. But here, the matter of reward is also repeatedly mentioned because the kingdom of the heavens is the reward.

Matthew 16:27-28 says, "For the Son of Man is to come in the glory of His Father and with His angels, and then He will repay each man according to his doings." God will reward or punish a saved person according to his doings. "Truly I say to you, There are some of those standing here who shall by no means taste death until they see the Son of Man coming in His kingdom." There are three facts here. First, man will be rewarded according to his works. The matter of reward is entirely based on works. Second, at what time will the reward be given out? It will be given out when Christ comes in the glory of His Father with His angels. When Christ comes in the glory of His Father with His angels, that will be the time for Him to establish His kingdom on the earth. Hence, it is only when the kingdom begins that the reward will begin. Third, here is a type which speaks of a fact. The transfiguration of the Lord on the mountain typifies His manifestation in glory in the coming kingdom. By that time some believers will be rewarded.

The verses in Matthew 6 which we just read regarding the reward for giving, the reward for prayer, and the reward for fasting all involve reward. Some think that the reward for prayer is God's answering of our prayer. But this is not all that is meant. The Lord Jesus said that we have to pray to our Father who is in secret, and our Father who sees in secret will repay us. It may be possible to interpret this as the Father answering our prayer. However, both in the first part when the Lord mentions alms-giving, and in the second part when He mentions fasting, He said, "And your Father who sees in secret will repay you." This repaying must refer to something in the future. Furthermore, the Lord said that we have to pray to the Father who sees in secret. It does not say that the Father hears in secret, but that He sees in secret. When God gives out the reward in the future, He gives according to what He sees. God sees with His eyes. Hence, the reward is in the future.

Revelation 11:15 says, "And the seventh angel trumpeted; and there were loud voices in heaven, saying, The kingdom of the world has become the kingdom of our Lord and of His Christ, and He will reign forever and ever." Verse 18 says, "And the nations became angry, and Your wrath came, and the time came for the dead to be judged, and the time to give the reward to Your slaves the prophets and to the saints and to those who fear Your name, to the small and to the great." This verse clearly shows us that when the Lord becomes King and the kingdom of the world becomes the kingdom of our Lord and of His Christ, that is the time for giving the reward to the saints, to the small and to the great. In other words, the time of the kingdom is the time of reward. Whenever the kingdom comes, the reward will come also.

There is a further point. The reward is the obtaining of the crown and the obtaining of the throne. Once a Western missionary told me, "If I cannot have the crown, at least I can have the kingdom." You can ask King Edward of England, if he loses his crown, will he still have the kingdom? What is a crown? It is not merely a hat beaten with gold and studded with diamonds. That kind of crown can be gained with a little money. What is a crown? A crown represents position in the kingdom. It also represents glory in the kingdom. If a crown is only a physical thing, it does not mean much. If one has money, he can make a golden one. If he does not have money, he can make a brass one or an iron one. Even if one is very poor, he can still make a crown out of cloth. In the future, it will not be a matter of one crown being bigger than the other in size, or one crown having more diamonds than the other. A crown stands for something. When one loses the crown, he loses the thing that the crown represents. We have to see that the crown is the symbol of the kingdom.

What is the throne? The Bible shows us that the twelve apostles will sit on twelve thrones. The crown is a reward for the overcomers, and the throne is also a reward for the overcomers. Hence, the throne is also a symbol of the kingdom. It represents position in the kingdom, authority in the kingdom, and glory in the kingdom. There is no such thing as losing the crown but still having the kingdom. Similarly, one cannot lose the throne but still have the kingdom. If one loses the throne, he will lose the kingdom. Similarly, if one loses the crown, he will lose the kingdom. The throne and the crown are not significant in themselves; they are there simply to represent the kingdom. In other words, the reward is the kingdom. The Bible clearly shows us that the reward is simply the kingdom.

JUDGMENT AT THE JUDGMENT SEAT OF CHRIST

How will God give us the reward? The time for us to be rewarded is when Christ comes again to execute judgment. Peter tells us that judgment begins from the house of God. In the future, God will judge the Christians first, before He judges the worldly people. Concerning what will God judge us? He will not judge us for eternal salvation or perdition. That judgment has been taken care of on the cross. All our sins have been judged on the cross, and the problem of eternal perdition has been resolved. But we Christians will be judged in the future. That judgment will determine whether or not we will participate in the kingdom. For some, not only will there not be participation in the kingdom, but there will be punishment as well. At that time, Christ will set up the judgment seat, and He will judge His believers at that judgment seat.

We will read two verses which are even clearer concerning this matter. Second Corinthians 5:10 says, "For we must all be manifested before the judgment seat of Christ, that each one may receive the things done through the body according to what he has practiced, whether good or bad." Every one of us who has believed in the Lord will be manifested before the judgment seat. The word "judgment seat" is *bema* in the original Greek. It means a raised platform. *Bema* is the place where matters are settled in the family. This verse says that we must all be manifested before the judgment seat that each may be recompensed according to what he has practiced. Eternal salvation or death is a matter of believing. But the judgment of a Christian is according to what he practices, whether good or evil. This is the judgment before the judgment seat.

Regarding the kingdom, there are a few things which we must know. Whether or not one can enter into the kingdom is one thing. Even if one can enter into the kingdom, there will still be a difference of position in the kingdom. If one cannot enter into the kingdom, he will go into outer darkness or will be chastised. Therefore, after we have believed in the Lord, though our good work cannot save us, it will determine our status in the kingdom. Thank God that the question of our eternal life or death is settled, but we will still be judged before the judgment seat of Christ. That judgment is not for determining our eternal life or death. It is for determining our position in the kingdom.

There are many other verses in the Bible that show us that believers will be judged by the Lord Jesus before the judgment seat of Christ. Among these verses, 1 Corinthians 3 shows us most clearly how we will be judged by the Lord before the judgment seat. First Corinthians 3:8 says, "Now he who plants and he who waters are one, but each will receive his own reward according to his own labor." The subject here is how each one will be rewarded according to his own labor. Verse 10 says, "According to the grace of God given to me, as a wise master builder I have laid a foundation, and another builds upon it. But let each man take heed how he builds upon it." The foundation is Jesus Christ. Each one's own labor is the way each one builds. The way we build is determined by the material we use. Verses 12-15 say, "But if anyone builds upon the foundation gold, silver, precious stones, wood, grass, stubble, the work of each will become manifest; for the day will declare it, because it is revealed by fire, and the fire itself will prove each one's work, of what sort it is. If anyone's work which he has built upon the foundation remains, he will receive a reward; if anyone's work is consumed, he will suffer loss, but he himself will be saved, yet so as through fire." This passage shows us that everyone who is building on this foundation is saved. The work which some build upon it will remain, and those ones will be rewarded. The work of some will not remain, and it will be consumed by fire. They will suffer loss, even though they will still be saved. Let us remember that there is still a judgment before us. That judgment will not determine whether or not we will perish, but it will determine whether we will receive a reward.

CHAPTER TWENTY-ONE

HOW GOD DEALS WITH THE BELIEVERS' SINS— THE QUALIFICATIONS FOR ENTERING INTO THE KINGDOM OF THE HEAVENS

We have made it clear that the kingdom is the time when God will reward the Christians according to their works. In the kingdom, the faithful believers will be rewarded, and the unfaithful believers will be punished. Many people think that if a Christian is unfaithful, although he may have to occupy a lower position, he will nevertheless make it into the kingdom. Many who do not understand God's word and God's work think that they are guaranteed an entrance into the kingdom of the heavens. They think that when the Lord Jesus comes to rule, there will merely be a distinction between higher and lower positions in the kingdom; no one will lose the kingdom of the heavens altogether. However, in the kingdom of the heavens, there is not only a distinction between higher and lower positions, but also the distinction between being allowed to enter and being kept out. The Bible shows us that there is a clear distinction between ten cities and five cities, between a large crown and a small one, and between a greater glory and a lesser one. As one star differs from another star, so also are the positions in the kingdom different. Not only is there the difference of lower and higher positions in the kingdom; there is also the distinction of being able or not able to get in.

DOING THE WILL OF THE FATHER

The Bible tells us of a very serious truth. Although someone may have eternal life, he may still be rejected from the kingdom of the heavens. One verse that speaks of this is Matthew 7:21: "Not every one who says to Me, Lord, Lord, will enter into the kingdom of the heavens, but he who does the will of My Father who is in the heavens." The persons in this verse all address the Lord as "Lord." The Lord will make a distinction between those disciples who can enter into the kingdom of the heavens and those who cannot. The Lord clearly shows us here that the condition for entering the kingdom of the heavens is doing the will of God. Although some have been saved and have called Him Lord, and although they have also done some works, without doing the will of God they nevertheless cannot enter into the kingdom of the heavens. The reward of the kingdom of the heavens is based on the obedience of man. If one is not faithful while living on the earth, though he will not lose eternal life, he will lose the kingdom of the heavens. When the time comes for the heavens to rule, that is, when the Lord Jesus comes the second time, some will not be able to enter the kingdom, but will lose it instead.

First, the Lord mentioned this matter in verse 21. Following this, in verses 22 and 23, He explained the matter to us in the way of a prophecy. There will be many, not only one or two, who will not do the will of God. "Many will say to Me in that day, Lord, Lord, was it not in Your name that we prophesied, and in Your name cast out demons, and in Your name did many works of power? And then I will declare to them: I never knew you. Depart from Me, you workers of lawlessness." Here the Lord Jesus tells us what will happen before the judgment seat. He says, "In that day." Hence, this does not refer to today, but to the future. There are many who work hard but do not see the light of God in their lives. When the time of the judgment seat comes, and when Christ begins to judge from the house of God, these Christians will have light for the first time. They will see that they are off in their standing and in their living.

In that day many will say before the Lord, "Was it not in Your name that we prophesied, and in Your name cast out demons, and in Your name did many works of power?" Within one sentence, the phrase "in Your name" is mentioned three

times. This proves that these ones are the Lord's. The fact
that they say, "Lord, Lord," proves that their standing is that
of a Christian. Not only do they say that they prophesy, cast
out demons, and do many works of power; they do these in
the Lord's name. The mentioning of "in Your name" three
times tells us of their relationship with the Lord.

Amazingly, the Lord tells them, "And then I will declare
to them: I never knew you." Because many do not understand
the meaning of these words, they think that these surely are
not saved ones. But if these are not saved ones, then the
Lord's word here would be meaningless. Matthew 7 is a conclusion to the sermon on the mount following the Lord's word
concerning the Beatitudes. These words on the mount were
spoken by the Lord Jesus to the disciples. After the Lord
went up the mountain, His disciples came before Him, and
He opened His mouth and taught them from chapter five to
chapter seven.

The Lord Jesus said that they should not call Him Lord
with their mouth only. If they call Him Lord, they should do
the will of the Father. Even if they have the outward works
of prophesying, casting out demons, and doing works of power,
these works must not replace the Father's will. Doing the
Father's will is one thing, whereas prophesying, casting out
demons, and doing works of power are another thing
altogether. Sometimes, one can prophesy, cast out demons,
and do works of power without doing the will of the Father.
We must remember that we should not only call Him Lord
with our mouth, but we should do the Father's will in our
walk as well. If the Lord were speaking about unsaved
persons, this word would lose its meaning altogether, for if
these are not saved ones, it would not matter much for the
disciples to listen or not to listen to His word. The disciples
may say that His word is for the unsaved ones, but they are
the saved ones; therefore whether or not they do the Father's
will, the Lord cannot deny knowing them. If this were the
case, then all the unsaved ones would be those who do not
do the will of God, and all the saved ones would be those
who do the will of God. This would take away the highest
meaning of these words.

The Lord Jesus must be warning the saved ones here by speaking about the saved ones. He cannot be warning the saved ones by speaking about the unsaved ones. Suppose one has a maid and two daughters, and suppose this one were to say to the younger daughter, "Do you see that maid? She is not born of me; I am beating her. You have to be obedient today. If you are not obedient, I will punish you in the same way I am punishing her." Is this word logical? A maid is not born of the family. If she becomes disobedient, she may be beaten. But the daughter of the family is not a maid. One cannot apply the way to deal with a maid to a daughter. The mother ought to say, "Last night I punished your sister because she was disobedient. Now be careful. If you are not obedient, I will punish you as well." The mother must take the sister as an example. The maid cannot be used for a comparison. There is no reason for the Lord to use unsaved ones as an example to show the disciples that they ought to do God's will. If He did, the disciples would rise up and say, "They are the unsaved ones, but we are the saved ones." If they were to say this, no one could say anything further.

What the Lord Jesus is saying is this: "Many people are God's children. They are saved and are the same as you are. They call Me 'Lord,' and they have done many works. But they are nevertheless shut outside the kingdom. For this reason you must be careful. You have to do the will of God." Only in this way will the disciples know that though they do many works, if they do not do the will of God, they will receive the same punishment. If He were speaking to the unsaved ones, there would no longer be the piercing element to His word. The Lord was warning us that only those who do the will of God can enter the kingdom. If one were to rely on his own work to come before God, the Lord Jesus would tell him, "I never knew you."

Let me give you another example. Suppose a judge's son drives carelessly and hits another car. He is taken by the police to the court for a hearing. The judge would ask, "Young man, what is your name? How old are you? Where do you live?" The son down at the stand may think, "You should know all these things better than I do." He may answer the first few questions. But after a while, he may shout to the father, "Father, don't you know me?" What should the judge do then? He may bang his gavel and say, "I do not know you. In my home, I know you. But in the court, I never knew you." If one sees the matter of the kingdom, he will realize that in the kingdom, it is not a matter of whether or not a person is saved and whether he is a child of God; what really matters is his work after becoming a believer. Suppose after you are saved, you are very zealous. Although you have not carried out God's will, you nevertheless prophesy, cast out demons, and do works of power in the Lord's name. If you come before the Lord asking to be admitted into the kingdom because of these unprincipled works, the Lord will say that He never knew you.

Why did the Lord say, "I never knew you"? The next sentence explains: "Depart from Me, you workers of lawlessness." Please remember that the Lord did not tell them to depart from eternal life. In the original Greek the meaning of workers of lawlessness is people who do not follow the rules, keep the law, or abide by the regulations. In the eyes of God, to do evil does not mean only to do bad things. It does not matter how much one has done; as long as he has not hearkened to God's demand, His judgment, and His sovereign arrangements, it is evil in God's eyes. If this word "lawlessness" were translated as "evil," as some versions have done, many would have the ground to argue. The problem here is not a matter of doing evil, but a matter of being unprincipled. What are the principles? The principles are God's word. But what is God's word? God's word is God's will. If you are not doing the will of God, no matter what you do, the Lord Jesus would say that you are lawless. Those who do things according to their own self will have no part in the kingdom of the heavens.

My purpose in saying these things is to show you the importance of a Christian's works. The Bible shows us clearly that after a person believes in the Lord, though he will never lose eternal life, he may lose his place and glory in the kingdom. If we do not do the will of God, but work according to our own will instead, we will be shut out of the kingdom.

We may think that prophesying, casting out demons, and doing works of power are most important, because we think that if we can do these things, we will be a marvelous person. But these things can never replace the will of God. All those who have never learned not to work for God are not worthy to work for God. Those who do not know how to stop their own work surely know nothing about God's will. Only those who know the will of God can stop working. God wants us first to obey His will and then to work. God does not want us to volunteer to work for Him. The more one knows about the will of the Lord, the more he will learn not to work carelessly. Thus, there is a big difference between working and doing the will of God. Today we may appreciate the works and may be interested in prophesying, casting out demons, and doing works of power. But one day, many will be awakened.

BUFFETING THE BODY TO PLEASE THE LORD

Another passage which some misinterpret as referring to perdition actually refers to the losing of the kingdom and the losing of the reward. First Corinthians 9:23-27 says, "And I do all things for the sake of the gospel that I may become a fellow partaker of it. Do you not know that those who run on a racecourse all run, but one receives the prize? Run in this way, that you may lay hold. And everyone who contends, exercises self-control in all things; they then, that they may receive a corruptible crown, but we, an incorruptible. I therefore run in this way, not as though without a clear aim; I box in this way, not as though beating the air; but I buffet my body and make it my slave, lest perhaps having preached to others, I myself may become disapproved." Paul feared that, having preached to others, he himself might be disapproved. Here Paul was saying that he could also be disapproved. What is the meaning of being disapproved here? And of what is one being disapproved? In these messages, we have emphasized the fact that in reading the Bible, one should pay attention to the context. Here we must also consider the context.

In verse 24 Paul likens himself to one who is running in

a race in which only one will get the prize. Therefore, the problem here is not a matter of salvation, but a matter of receiving the prize. Paul is talking about how a saved one can receive the prize; he is not talking about how an unsaved one can be saved. Only the ones who are saved, who have believed in the Lord Jesus, who are reborn, and who have become the children of God are qualified to enter the race. Only the children of God can run in the race and pursue the prize that God intends for us to gain. If someone is not a child of God, he will not be qualified even to enter the race. Nowhere does the Bible say that salvation is gained by our running the race. The Bible never says that if someone is able to run, he will be saved. If that were so, then very few could be saved, and salvation would be dependent on works. The Bible says that the prize comes from the running; God has placed us on a racecourse for us to run the race.

What is the prize? Verse 25 says, "And everyone who contends exercises self-control in all things; they then, that they may receive a corruptible crown, but we, an incorruptible." Here it says that the prize is a crown. We have mentioned that the crown signifies glory and the kingdom. Therefore, the word "disapproved" does not refer to the losing of salvation. The word "disapproved" means to fail to receive the crown and the prize. If Paul could be disapproved, then we all have the possibility of being disapproved. If Paul had the possibility of losing his prize and losing his crown, then each one of us also has the possibility of losing the prize and the crown.

Verse 26 indicates the reason for being disapproved: "I therefore run in this way, not as though without a clear aim; I box in this way, not as though beating the air." Paul had a purpose and a direction. He was not beating the air. His goal and direction were what he said in 2 Corinthians 5, that he was ambitious to be well-pleasing to the Lord. Whether he would live or die on this earth, his desire was to please the Lord. How did he run in the race? He did not run in a loose way. He had a definite direction and a definite goal. He was not beating the air. He did not simply do whatever others told him to do. Nor did he do something simply because the need was there. If he were to work according to the need, he would have to run day and night, for the need was too great. We are not for the work, but for pleasing the Lord.

If we want to receive the prize, what should we do? "But I buffet my body and make it my slave." Many would place their own bodies above the prize. Many would place their own bodies above the will of God. But Paul said that he subjected his body; he was able to control it. Paul could control the lust of his body, the excessive demands of his body, and the desires of his body. He did not let his body get on top. He said that he buffeted his body and made it his slave. Whether or not a Christian can please the Lord depends upon whether he can control his body. Many people cannot control their own bodies. Whenever a little stimulus comes to their body, all kinds of sins result. We must see that all those who cannot control their own bodies will lose their prize and their crown. Although they can preach the gospel to others, they themselves will be disapproved.

We believers are saved once and for all and will never lose our salvation. But when the Lord Jesus returns in His glory to rule the earth, He will not give crowns to everyone. In the new heaven and new earth, although every saved one will receive the same glory, when the Lord Jesus comes to rule on this earth for a thousand years, some will lose their prize, their authority, and their glory. Some will not be able to enter the kingdom and will not be able to receive a crown.

The Lord's word is very clear concerning the matters of salvation and eternal life: both are totally of grace. Moreover, whether or not one can enter into the kingdom of the heavens depends upon his works. We have just seen that we have to do the will of God. Here we see that we have to buffet our own body. We may do many works outwardly, but as long as we do not restrict our body, we will not be allowed into the kingdom.

In the Bible there seems to be a fixed number of crowns. Revelation 3:11 says, "I come quickly; hold fast what you have that no one take your crown." Some who do not understand the Bible do not know the difference between a reward and a gift. Neither do they know the difference between the crown and God's salvation. They think that salvation can be taken away from them. The word "take" here does not refer to salvation but to the crown. One can be saved yet still lose the crown. There was a very sensational headline in the news recently. A certain king of a certain country had lost his crown. If a saved one does not hold fast to what he has, if he does not keep the words of endurance of the Lord Jesus, and if he forsakes the name of the Lord Jesus, he will lose his crown some day. If you are loose, and if you do not hold fast, you will lose your crown. Someone else might take away your crown from you.

Revelation 2:10 has a word similar to this: "Be faithful unto death, and I will give you the crown of life." Here it does not say give life, but give the crown of life. Life is obtained through faith; it is not obtained through faithfulness. If a person does not have faith, he cannot have life. But if a person is unfaithful after he has life, he will lose the crown of life. Hence, if a Christian does not have good works after being saved, though he will not lose life, he will nevertheless lose the crown.

BUILDING WITH GOLD, SILVER, AND PRECIOUS STONES

The clearest passage in the Bible about the reward is 1 Corinthians 3:14-15: "If anyone's work which he has built upon the foundation remains, he will receive a reward; if anyone's work is consumed, he will suffer loss, but he himself will be saved." This shows us clearly what a Christian cannot lose and what he can lose. Once a person is saved, he is surely saved forever. But whether or not such a one will receive a reward cannot be decided today. A Christian's eternal salvation is settled already. But the future reward is a question that is still pending. It is decided by how one builds upon the foundation of the Lord Jesus. Our salvation does not depend on how we build. It depends only on how the Lord builds. If His work is perfect, we are surely saved. However, whether or not we will receive the reward or suffer loss depends on our own building work. If one builds with gold, silver, and precious stones, things with eternal value, upon the foundation of the Lord Jesus, he will surely receive a reward. But if he builds with wood, hay, and stubble, he will not receive a reward before God. He may have much before man, yet he will not have much before God. This shows us that it is possible for a man to lose his reward and to have his work burned away.

Let me repeat this. Thank God that the matter of our eternal salvation was decided over nineteen hundred years ago. When the Son of God was hung on the cross, the question of our salvation was settled. But whether or not we will receive the reward depends on how we behave. The truth of the gospel is very balanced. Salvation rests totally with the Lord Jesus. The giving of salvation depends absolutely on the Lord Jesus. However, whether or not one can obtain his reward depends on his own building work. Man must believe, and he also must work. This work is not his own work, but what the Holy Spirit has worked out in him. Here we see that it is possible for us to lose our reward. It is also possible for us to be disapproved for the kingdom and to have our crown taken away. It seems that our position in the kingdom is never settled; it is subject to change and not assured.

HOLDING FAST THE BOAST OF HOPE

Hebrews 3:6 gives us a similar word. "But Christ was faithful as a Son over His house, whose house we are if indeed we hold fast the boldness and the boast of hope firm to the end." Here it seems uncertain as to whether or not we are His house. The apostle said that we are His house if we hold fast the boldness and the boast of hope firm to the end. What is this house and this hope? This blessed hope is nothing other than that of the Lord Jesus returning in glory to set up His kingdom on the earth. If a Christian has such a hope, knowing that the Lord Jesus will come again to set up His kingdom in glory, and knowing that all those faithful ones who do the will of God will reign with the Lord, if such a one holds fast to this, he will be His house. Today we are His house already. We are all living stones built into a spiritual house. This is what Peter has told us (1 Pet. 2:5). But how we will fare in the future kingdom depends on how we hold fast. This matter cannot be decided once and for all.

There are many verses in the Bible concerning this, and all are very clear. The problem of eternity is totally settled, but the matter of position and reward in the kingdom depends on how we hold fast today.

BEING THE MORE DILIGENT TO MAKE THE CALLING AND SELECTION FIRM

We come to 2 Peter 1:10: "Therefore, brothers, be the more diligent to make your calling and selection firm, for doing these things you shall by no means ever stumble." If one does not know the truth about selection, he will not see that this refers to the hope of the kingdom being firm. Here it says that a person's selection and calling is not necessarily firm. Does this mean that a person will become unsaved again? No, it does not, because Romans 11 clearly tells us that the calling of God is irrevocable (11:29). Here it is not talking only about calling, but selection as well. Peter put calling and selection together. The Bible says many times that many are called, but few are chosen. Except for one place which I am not absolutely sure about, all the other places refer to many being saved and few obtaining a reward. Hence, the selection here refers to the position in the kingdom.

Peter said, "For doing these things you shall by no means ever stumble." These are the things mentioned in verses 5-7, such as faith, virtue, knowledge, self-control, endurance, godliness, and love. If we do these things, we will never stumble. This is the same as saying that if we are the more diligent, our calling and selection will be firm. These are parallel expressions. The first of these parallel expressions says that we should be diligent to make our calling and selection firm. The second of these parallel expressions says that by doing these, we will never stumble.

Verse 11 says, "For in this way the entrance into the eternal kingdom of our Lord and Savior Jesus Christ will be richly and bountifully supplied to you." The Bible shows us that the kingdom of Christ is eternal. But some will enter it only in eternity future, whereas others will enter it during the millennium. The ruling of Christ begins with the millennial kingdom. Therefore, Revelation 11:15 says, "And the seventh angel trumpeted; and there were loud voices in heaven, saying, The kingdom of the world has become the kingdom of our Lord and of His Christ, and He will reign forever and ever." This verse shows us that the kingdom of Christ is linked to eternity future; it lasts forever and ever. However, it begins at the trumpeting of the seventh angel, that is, at the beginning of the tribulation. When Christ begins His reign, some will enter the kingdom. They will not only enter in, but will be richly and bountifully supplied an entrance. Therefore, to make our calling and selection firm is to be richly and bountifully supplied with an entrance into this eternal kingdom.

One can see that salvation has been settled, but that the entrance into the kingdom has not yet been settled. Once a Christian believes in the Lord Jesus, he can immediately praise the Lord because he knows that the question of eternal life or death is settled. However, after one believes, there are experiences ahead of him; he still has the kingdom before him and a future glory waiting for him. Some will obtain these things: the kingdom, the crown, the glory, and the reward; whereas others will not obtain them. Some will enter into the kingdom of Christ; others will not be able to enter in. Some will not only enter in, but will be richly and bountifully supplied an entrance into the kingdom of Christ. This does not mean that those who cannot enter the kingdom of Christ are not saved. But it does mean that their reward and glory are taken away. Hence, we need to run and strive. Our being able to reign with Jesus the Nazarene in the future depends on how we strive today.

ENTERING THE KINGDOM
TO SHARE IN CHRIST'S GLORY

I wonder if you have ever thought of the kind of glory with which God will reward Christ in the millennium for what He suffered nineteen hundred years ago. A reward must match a suffering. If a man is brought to the lowest position, his reward must be the greatest. Suppose your house is burned or you have encountered a grave danger, and a servant in your house risked everything and nearly lost his life trying

QUALIFICATIONS FOR ENTERING THE KINGDOM 415

to save you. How would you reward him? Would you say, "I reward you with twenty cents"? No one would do this. The reward has to match the suffering. Christ has glorified God in such a way and has died such a death on the cross. How shall God reward Christ in the future? And how shall He glorify Christ?

The kingdom is the time when Christ and the Christians will receive glory together. The kingdom is the time when God will reward Christ. At that time, we will have a portion there as well. Whether or not we would be counted worthy to receive the Lord's glory depends absolutely on the results of our personal walk and work. There is no question of worthiness in the new heaven and new earth. But in the kingdom only those who are worthy will receive the glory. The Lord has suffered persecution, difficulties, and shame. If we suffer persecution, difficulties, and shame today in the same way, we will share a portion with Him in the coming kingdom.

CHAPTER TWENTY-TWO

HOW GOD DEALS
WITH THE BELIEVERS' SINS—
DISCIPLINE IN THE KINGDOM

(1)

SUFFERING GOD'S DISCIPLINE IN THE COMING AGE

The Bible tells us that the Lord disciplines us because He loves us (Heb. 12:6). When man loves, he overlooks. But when God loves, He disciplines. When man loves, he is loose. But when God loves, He is serious. If God had not loved us, He would not have sent His Son to die for our sins on the cross. Similarly, if God does not love us, He would not discipline us. God's disciplining love is the same as His saving love, which caused Him to send His Son to die for us on the cross. It was His love that caused His Son to die on our behalf. It is also His love that disciplines us. Every Christian knows that there is no contradiction between God's discipline and God's grace. On the contrary, God's discipline manifests God's grace. Although we have seen that a man cannot perish again after he is saved, we can never say that such a one will never suffer God's discipline. Now the question is whether God's discipline is confined to this age or whether it will be found in the coming age as well. This is a question that many people have never considered. We will take a look at this matter.

The Bible shows us that God's discipline is not restricted to this age only. It is also found in the next age. Many people have confined God's discipline to this age. But you cannot find the basis for such a teaching in the Bible. In terms of the experience of Christians, there is surely the possibility for discipline in the next age. Many have not been disciplined in this age. Although they are God's children, they have not lived a consecrated life in this age. They do whatever they want and do many things in disobedience throughout their lives and until their death. Although some have been zealous for the Lord and have worked and have even experienced many miracles and works of power outwardly, these things are all done according to their own will and contrary to God's purpose. Some even have obvious sins and specific transgressions. But we do not see much discipline in these ones. On the contrary, they live peacefully and depart from this world in peace. However, in addition to losing the reward, these people will be disciplined in the kingdom. They will experience specific discipline from God. Hence, experientially speaking, if a Christian lives on earth today without checking his lust and instead loves the world and walks in his own ways, he will be disciplined in the coming age. We have ample evidence of this from the Bible.

THE PURPOSE OF DISCIPLINE
BEING FOR THE CLEANSING

According to the Word of God, discipline is for cleansing. Man is defiled; therefore, he needs to be cleansed. In the Bible there is not only one kind of cleansing. The first cleansing is the cleansing of the blood, that is, the cleansing by the blood of the Lord Jesus. The Bible mentions the cleansing of the blood over three hundred times. Here we will mention only two verses. Hebrews 9:22 says, "And almost all things are purified by blood according to the law, and without shedding of blood there is no forgiveness." This verse speaks of the purification by the blood. Hebrews 1:3 says, "Who, being the effulgence of His glory and the impress of His substance and upholding and bearing all things by the word of His power, having made purification of sins, sat down on the right hand of the Majesty on high." Here we can translate "having made cleansing of sins." In the Bible we see the cleansing of our sins by the blood of the Lord Jesus. After He cleansed our sins, He ascended to the heights and sat down on the right hand of the Majesty on high. This is the first kind of cleansing in the Bible.

However, although many people have received the cleansing of the blood of the Lord Jesus, they still have many filthy thoughts while living on earth. They are still very much defiled by the world and have many fleshly sins. Because there are these many other things, God uses other means to cleanse us. This is the way of cleansing by discipline and chastisement which we will now talk about.

In John 15:2 the Lord says, "Every branch in Me that does not bear fruit, He takes it away; and every branch that bears fruit, He prunes it that it may bear more fruit." The pruning here is a cleansing. God cuts away the unnecessary, unimportant, and hindering elements that the branches may bear more fruit. This is God's discipline. Hence, the purpose of God's discipline is not for destroying us but for perfecting us, so that we may become more worthy of God's glory, of God's holiness, and of the righteousness that is set before us.

Thus, there are two lines and two cleansings in God's Word. One is the cleansing by the blood of the Lord Jesus. The other is the cleansing by God which comes through our environment, our family, our personal health, or our job. If we indulge in what we should not indulge in or refuse to cut off what we should cut off, God's disciplining hand will be upon us in our environment.

THE CLEANSING IN THE COMING AGE

Is this cleansing discipline from God restricted to this age only, or is it found also in the coming age? From the Bible we know that death never changes anyone. Nowhere in the Bible are we shown a case of a man changed by death. We know that in the future we will be with God forever. In eternity we will be the same as the Lord; we will be holy, even as the Lord is holy. But can we say that today we are as holy as the Lord is? Can we say that we are worthy to be with the Lord for eternity? The blood of the Lord Jesus has cleansed us and that the record of our sins has been wiped away. This is a fact. But subjectively speaking, do we have Christ living in us experientially? Have we allowed the resurrected Christ to live out from us? Our walk today is far too different from what our walk must be in eternity; the two are too far apart. Today we come far short of the Lord's holiness, righteousness, and glory. Many Christians today are still full of sins and filth.

So then, we have a problem. If things are so bad today but will be so good in the future, if things are so imperfect today but will be so perfect in the future, when will the change take place? Somewhere along the way there must be a change. If you are not perfect today, but will be perfect in that day, when will such a change take place? In eternity, when we are with God and the Lamb in the New Jerusalem, we will be in the light as God is in the light. But when will we become such ones? The human concept is that when we die we will change. But the Bible never tells us that physical death will make a person holy. This was a doctrine that was preached five or six hundred years ago. But the Bible never says that death can change a person. If death could change a Christian, then death could also change an unsaved person. But death never changes anyone. The slothful servant is still slothful when he is resurrected. The foolish virgins are still foolish when they wake up. When they wake up, their slothfulness and foolishness have not gone away. If a man is not changed in this age but will be different in the new heaven and new earth, and if death does not cause a person to change, then when does the change occur? The Bible shows us clearly that in the coming age there will be discipline, and this discipline will prune and cleanse us.

SOME SERVANTS OF GOD
TO BE JUDGED IN THE COMING AGE

We need to look at a few verses concerning this future discipline. Luke 12:45-48 says, "But if that slave says in his heart, My master is delaying his coming, and begins to beat the male servants and the female servants and to eat and to drink and become drunk, the master of that slave will come on a day when he does not expect him and at an hour which he does not know, and will cut him asunder, and will appoint his portion with the unbelievers. And that slave who knew his master's will and did not prepare or do according to his will, will receive many lashes; but he who did not know, yet did things worthy of stripes, will receive few lashes. But to

DISCIPLINE IN THE KINGDOM

every one to whom much has been given, much will be required from him; and to whom much has been committed, they will ask of him all the more."

The first thing in these verses that we have to decide is whether or not the slave belongs to the Lord. Is he a Christian? Is he saved? Surely the slave is a saved one. How can I say this? First, in the New Testament God never considers those who do not belong to Him as His slaves. In going from the Old Testament to the New Testament age, first, man is a slave and then becomes a son. Thus, in the Old Testament there are many unsaved slaves. But in the New Testament the order is reversed. If a man is not God's son, he is not qualified to be God's slave. All slaves of God are sons in the New Testament. Therefore, the slave spoken of here is surely a saved one.

There is a second proof that the slave in Luke 12:45-48 is saved. The proof is in the previous verses. Verses 42-44 say, "And the Lord said, Who then is the faithful and prudent steward, whom the master will set over his service to give them their portion of food at the proper time? Blessed is that slave whom his master, when he comes, will find so doing. Truly I tell you that he will set him over all his possessions." Is the slave in these verses the same one as the slave in verses 45 and 46? Or are there two slaves? There is only one slave. The slave in verses 43 and 44 is the one in verse 45. The same person can be a good slave as well as a bad slave. This slave can have two different minds. If he is faithful to the charge of the master of the house and would give to the household their portion of food at the proper time, the master will reward him well and will set him over all his possessions. But if the slave says in his heart, "The master is delaying his coming; I can act any way I want," and he begins to beat the male servants and the female servants, the master will come and judge his sins. This proves that a saved person can both be a good slave and a bad slave.

If a saved person has unfortunately become an evil slave, what will his end be? Verse 46 says, "The master of that slave will come on a day when he does not expect him and at an hour which he does not know, and will cut him asunder,

and will appoint his portion with the unbelievers." Does this
chastisement occur in this age or in the age to come? What
does the day and hour which he does not know refer to? They
must refer to the time when the Lord will come back. This
is something in the future. The Lord says that a slave can
be faithful or unfaithful and that an unfaithful slave will not
only miss the reward, but will also be condemned and receive
a definite punishment. Verses 47 and 48 are based on the
words of verse 46. They tell us of the future of those who
belong to the Lord and who work for the Lord. "And that
slave who knew his master's will and did not prepare or do
according to his will, will receive many lashes; but he who
did not know, yet did things worthy of stripes, will receive
few lashes. But to every one to whom much has been given,
much will be required from him; and to whom much has been
committed, they will ask of him all the more." These verses
do not say that those who do not know will not receive any
lashes; they only say that they will receive few lashes. There
will still be the lashes. God does not let those who do not
know get by, because His word is here. Those who know have
to be responsible before God; those who do not know and who
have done things worthy of lashes will still receive lashes,
yet they will receive few lashes. Everyone to whom much has
been given, much will be required from him; and to whom
much has been committed, they will ask of him all the more.
This is the principle of God's future chastisement. Luke
12:47-48 settles for us the question of future chastisement
of Christians before God.

My friends, I am here preaching the gospel of grace. When
a man is saved, he is saved forever. This is an immutable
fact. However, after we are saved, if our conduct is unbecom-
ing of Christians, we will be chastised in the future. I am
only a preacher of the Word of God. I am responsible to speak
only what the Bible says. I am not responsible for what the
Bible ought to say. Today some may ask why Christians need
to be chastised in the future. I do not know. You can ask the
Lord for yourself. I am only saying what the Bible has said.
This is the Lord's word.

Let us read Colossians 3:23-25. "Whatever you do, work

from the soul as to the Lord and not to men, knowing that from the Lord you will receive the inheritance as recompense. You serve the Lord Christ. For he who does unrighteously will receive what he unrighteously did, and there is no respect of persons." The context of this passage makes it clear that these verses refer to Christians, not to unbelievers. The preceding verses speak of how a Christian should be a wife, a husband, a father or a mother, a son or a daughter, a master or a slave. Then Paul says that if a Christian does unrighteously, he will receive what he unrighteously did, because there is no respect of persons. This shows us clearly that a Christian's recompense comes at the judgment seat of Christ. If he does unrighteously today, he will receive a recompense according to what he has done unrighteously. If he acts righteously, he will receive his recompense according to his righteousness. Hence, we cannot say that Christians will not receive a certain amount of discipline and chastisement.

RECEIVING THE THINGS DONE THROUGH THE BODY

Now let us read 2 Corinthians 5:10. "For we must all be manifested before the judgment seat of Christ, that each one may receive the things done through the body according to what he has practiced, whether good or bad." All Bible readers know that the judgment seat of Christ is in the air. Hence, those standing before the judgment seat are those who have been raptured. And who can be raptured? The Bible tells us that only Christians can be raptured. Those who are not Christians cannot be raptured. If a man is not saved and is not a child of God, he is not even qualified to be judged at this judgment. This is God's judgment within His own family. Here it tells us what we will be faced with at the future judgment seat of Christ. We will be recompensed for the things done through the body. In other words, we will be recompensed for the things done in the body, that is, for the things we have done while living on earth, whether good or bad. If you do good in the body, you will receive a good reward. If you do evil in the body, you will receive the recompense of evil. The Word of God shows us clearly that at the judgment seat those who do well will receive a reward and that those

THE GOSPEL OF GOD

who do not do well will lose their reward and will be
recompensed according to their evil.

Because there is a future judgment, the apostle Paul
prayed concerning mercy in the future. Second Timothy 1:18
says, "May the Lord grant him to find mercy from the Lord
in that day. And in how many things he served me in Ephesus,
you know best." Paul expressed the wish that Onesiphorus
would find mercy from the Lord in that day. If a Christian
will at most lose his reward in the future when he stands
before the judgment seat and will not be punished or
disciplined, then this word is meaningless. Paul hoped that
the Lord would be merciful to Onesiphorus at His judgment,
because Onesiphorus had helped Paul so much and had
propagated the gospel with him. If there were any wrongs
that Onesiphorus had done, Paul hoped that the Lord would
be merciful to him. Hence, we see that Christians need not
only forgiveness, but also God's mercy at the time of judgment
at the beginning of the millennium; otherwise, they will fall
under God's chastisement.

In 2 Timothy 4 there is another verse which we should
read. Verse 16 says, "At my first defense no one was with me
to support me, but all abandoned me. May it not be counted
against them." This is another prayer. While Paul was in
Asia, the whole of Asia abandoned him. While he was before
the king being judged, many Christians were fearful of death
and hid off to the side. Yet even though they had abandoned
him, Paul prayed that this sin would not be counted against
them. Hence, we see that in the future God will still judge
our sins. Paul prayed here that this sin would not be counted
against them. There is enough light in the Bible to show us
that if a saved person is not disciplined for his loose conduct
in this age, or if he does not repent after discipline, he will
not only lose his reward but will also be chastised in a definite
way.

In Matthew 12 the Lord Jesus specifically mentions
blaspheming the Holy Spirit. All sins can be forgiven. All the
words spoken against the Son of Man can be forgiven. But
the sin of blaspheming the Holy Spirit cannot be forgiven.
There will not be forgiveness in this age, and there will not

be forgiveness in the next age (v. 32). In the Bible the coming age always refers to the kingdom. In the original language the word for age is *aion,* not *cosmos.* If the word were *cosmos,* it would refer to the organization of the world. But since it is *aion,* it refers to a time span. Hence, it is translated *age.* Today is the age of grace. The next age is the age when the Lord will come to reign for a thousand years. When you read Matthew 12, you see that the forgiveness of sins is divided into two time periods. Some sins are forgiven in this age, and some sins are forgiven in the coming age. Some people, through discipline, are forgiven in this age. Some people may not have done well today, but they will be forgiven in the kingdom. Some people are forgiven when they are saved, but their subsequent sins will not be forgiven in the kingdom; they will be chastised severely instead. This is the biblical teaching concerning chastisement. Chastisement for the Christian in this age is clear enough. Some sinning Christians whose problems are not solved before God today will receive chastisement in the future.

THE KINGDOM BEING
THE TIME OF THE FUTURE CHASTISEMENT

When exactly will the future chastisement be? It is clear that there will be chastisement in the future after the Lord comes back, but when after the Lord's return will it be? Let us consider three ages in the Bible. The present age can be called the age of grace. It can also be called the age of the gospel or the age of the church. The coming age can be called the age of the kingdom or the millennial age, because that age will only last a thousand years (Rev. 20:6). After that age, there is yet another age, which is an eternal age. It is the age of the new heaven and new earth.

The Bible presents to us these three ages. The age of the church is the age of grace because God's grace and love are manifested in it. In this age God saves the unrighteous ones and causes man to receive the grace of the Lord Jesus. Everything in this age is of grace. The coming age is the age of righteousness. The eternal age is also an age of grace. Today is an age of grace, and the new heaven and new earth is also an age of grace. But the kingdom is all righteousness. If you are not clear about these ages, your reading of the Bible, theology, and biblical understanding will be all wrong. Both the church age and the age of the new heaven and new earth are ages of grace. But the millennial age is a parenthetical age specially prepared by God for the reward of the faithful ones and the chastisement of the sinful ones. That is a special period.

Both the New Testament and the Old Testament tell us that in this period, God deals with man in righteousness (Psa. 72:2; 85:10-13; 96:13; 97:2; Isa. 11:5; 26:9; 33:5; 62:1; Jer. 33:15; Dan. 7:27). We can quote at least two hundred verses from the Old and New Testaments concerning the righteous judgment in the kingdom.

What is the difference between the kingdom and the new heaven and new earth? The Bible makes a clear distinction between the two. Let us consider Revelation 19:6-8. "And I heard as it were the voice of a great multitude and like the sound of many waters and like the sound of mighty thunders, saying, Hallelujah! For the Lord our God the Almighty reigns." Please notice that here is the beginning of the kingdom. "Let us rejoice and exult, and let us give the glory to Him, for the marriage of the Lamb has come, and His wife has made herself ready. And it was given to her that she should be clothed in fine linen, bright and clean; for the fine linen is the righteousnesses of the saints." Here we read that fine linen is given to the bride. But though it is given, it is nevertheless of righteousness. The fine linen is the righteousness in the actions of the believers. In the original language, the righteousnesses mentioned here refer to righteousness in actions. The word has the sense of actions. Hence, it refers to our own righteous acts.

Now let us read 20:4-6. "And I saw thrones, and they sat upon them, and judgment was given to them. And I saw the souls of those who had been beheaded because of the testimony of Jesus and because of the word of God, and of those who had not worshipped the beast nor his image, and had not received the mark on their forehead and on their hand; and they lived and reigned with Christ for a thousand years. The rest of the dead did not live again until the thousand years were completed. This is the first resurrection. Blessed and holy is he who has part in the first resurrection; over these the second death has no authority, but they will be priests of God and of Christ and will reign with Him for a thousand years." These verses tell us who will be the kings who reign with Christ a thousand years. The kingdom is not for everybody. The kingdom is only for the martyrs. It is only for those who reject Satan and Antichrist. Only these ones can reign for a thousand years. Hence, only the martyrs can reign; only those who reject Satan and Antichrist will be kings. This proves to us that the millennial kingdom is not given as a free gift, but is obtained through good works before God. Although in other passages we see other kinds of people reigning, in Revelation we see that there must be specific righteousness before there can be participation in the marriage feast of the Lamb. Only those who are the martyrs can be the kings. Without having the particular righteousness and without being martyred, no one can have a part in the kingship. This is the millennium.

THE AGE OF THE NEW HEAVEN AND NEW EARTH

Let us now consider Revelation 21. Verses 1 through 7 say, "And I saw a new heaven and a new earth; for the first heaven and the first earth passed away, and the sea is no more. And I saw the holy city, New Jerusalem, coming down out of heaven from God, prepared as a bride adorned for her husband. And I heard a loud voice out of the throne, saying, Behold, the tabernacle of God is with men, and He will tabernacle with them, and they will be His peoples, and God Himself will be with them and be their God. And He will wipe away every tear from their eyes; and death will be no more, nor will there be sorrow or crying or pain anymore; for the former things have passed away. And He who sits on the throne said, Behold, I make all things new. And He said, Write, for these words are faithful and true. And He said to me, They have come to pass. I am the Alpha and the Omega, the Beginning and the End. I will give to him who thirsts from the spring of the water of life freely. He who overcomes will inherit these things, and I will be God to him, and he will be a son to Me."

The description of the kingdom in Revelation 19 and 20 is entirely different from the description of the new heaven and new earth in chapter twenty-one. When describing the kingdom, the Bible speaks about what man has done. But when it describes the new heaven and new earth, there is no more mention of what man has done. From chapter twenty-one on, the Bible simply speaks of what God has done. God said that He has made all things new. God said that the first heaven and the first earth have passed away and that the sea is no more. All these are done by God. The tabernacle of God will be with men. He shall tabernacle with men. We are His people; God Himself will dwell with us and will be our God. He will wipe away all our tears, so that we will have no more death, sorrow, crying, or pain, for all the former things will have passed away, and all things will have been made new. God said all these words are faithful. He said that He is the Alpha and the Omega. Man has no place here at all. These verses go on and on, telling us what God has done. There is no condition or demand. If you wish to know how to obtain such a wonderful new heaven and new earth, just listen to His word: "And He said to me, They have come to pass. I am the Alpha and the Omega, the Beginning and the End" (v. 6a). In other words, everything is done by God. "I will give to him who thirsts from the spring of the water of life freely" (v. 6b). After all these things have been said, everything is summed up in one sentence: "I will give to him who thirsts from the spring of the water of life freely." As long as there is the thirst, as long as there is the need, God will give from the spring of the water of life freely. This is grace. Grace is to give from the spring of the water of life freely. The new heaven and the new earth is of grace. God is the Alpha and the Omega, the beginning and the end. The new heaven and the new earth are absolutely from Him.

The next verse says, "He who overcomes will inherit these things." Who are these overcomers to whom John refers? The overcomers here are different from the overcomers in the epistles to the seven churches at the beginning of Revelation.

Here, by the use of the term *overcomers,* a distinction is being made between the worldly people and the Christians. The distinction here is not between one kind of Christian and another kind of Christian. The overcoming in the first three chapters of Revelation is the overcoming by some Christians among other Christians. But the overcoming in chapter twenty-one is the overcoming by the Christians among the worldly people. How can we drink of the water of life? It is by faith. Those who believe can drink. In order to drink of the water of life freely, we have to believe. It is faith that enables us to overcome the world. Compared to the worldly people, every Christian is an overcomer. But compared to other Christians, many Christians are failing ones. Compared to those in the world, we are all overcomers because we have a faith before God that the worldly people do not have. Those who overcome and those who drink of the water of life will inherit these things, and God will be God to them, and they will be sons to God.

Chapter twenty-two also mentions the new heaven and new earth. Verses 1 through 5 say, "And he showed me a river of water of life, bright as crystal, proceeding out of the throne of God and of the Lamb in the middle of its street. And on this side and on that side of the river was the tree of life, producing twelve fruits, yielding its fruit each month; and the leaves of the tree are for the healing of the nations. And there will no longer be a curse. And the throne of God and of the Lamb will be in it, and His slaves will serve Him; and they will see His face, and His name will be on their forehead. And night will be no more; and they have no need of the light of a lamp and of the light of the sun, for the Lord God will shine upon them; and they will reign forever and ever." The main thing in the New Jerusalem is the river of water of life. This river proceeds from the throne of God and of the Lamb. Because it is the river of life, there is the tree of life, with the fruit of life growing. In Revelation 22, after everything has been said, one thing is prominent, the river of life. This river of the water of life flows throughout the city. How can we enjoy the river of the water of life? At the end of Revelation, after the kingdom is over and after the church is over, verse 17 says, "And the Spirit and the bride say, Come! And let him who hears say, Come! And let him who is thirsty come; let him who wills take the water of life freely." In other words, everyone is welcomed into the new heaven and new earth. In the new heaven and new earth there is a throne, and beneath the throne there is a river. The river comes forth from God and has the throne as its source. The throne is the center of the new heaven and new earth.

Furthermore, the word *Lamb* is never mentioned related to the kingdom. But in the new heaven and new earth, the Lamb is indeed mentioned. The throne is of God and of the Lamb (22:1); the Lord God Almighty and the Lamb are the temple of the city (21:22); and the Lamb is the lamp of the city (21:23). That the Lamb is mentioned related to the new heaven and new earth indicates that this will be an age of grace. When we come to the end of Revelation, the church, the kingdom, and the tribulation are no longer mentioned. Instead, we find only that all who are thirsty can come and take of the water of life freely. This means that you are invited to the new heaven and new earth. Everything is free. And that it is free means that it is of grace. Therefore, the new heaven and new earth are entirely different from the kingdom. The new heaven and new earth are freely given to us. According to the teaching of Revelation, we can say that in the new heaven and new earth God deals with man in grace. In the kingdom, however, He deals with the Christians in righteousness. Therefore, we have to admit that it is in the kingdom that God chastises us. In the new heaven and new earth everything is received freely.

In this we see the relationship between today and the future. If we love the world today, walk by the flesh, and live a loose life, in the age to come we will be chastised by God. But if we love the Lord today and forsake everything for the Lord's sake, we will receive God's grace and His reward. This is the biblical teaching concerning these three ages. I am not responsible for what I am speaking here. I am only speaking God's Word. God's Word says that in the coming age there will be these things. God Himself is responsible for all of His own words. I only know that the Son of God has said these words. It is true that a man can enjoy eternal life today. But the kingdom is the time when God will deal with His children. If you live a loose life today, you will be disciplined in the future. Hence, we have eternal security, but we also have temporary danger. We have the security of the new heaven and new earth. But we also have the peril of the kingdom. In the kingdom we may suffer severe punishment and chastisement. Whereas salvation is settled by the work of the Lord Jesus, reward is judged by one's work. Salvation comes by the work of the Lord Jesus. Reward comes by our own work. We are rewarded because we obey the will of God and walk not according to our own will. May we treasure the grace that we have received, and may we receive the warning from God and pursue after the reward of the kingdom.

CHAPTER TWENTY-THREE

HOW GOD DEALS WITH THE BELIEVERS' SINS— DISCIPLINE IN THE KINGDOM

(2)

RECEIVING LIFE IN THE KINGDOM IN THE COMING AGE

When we preach the gospel, we tell others that we receive eternal life through believing in Jesus Christ. If a person believes in Him, he will have eternal life. Everyone who understands the Word of God knows that in the church age, as soon as a man believes, he has eternal life. This is our message. But the question now is this: When is this eternal life manifested, revealed, and enjoyed? Today our minds and spirits are constantly being harassed by death. Satan is still very strong. So when will the eternal life be fully manifested? Will it be in the new heaven and new earth? Or will it be in the kingdom? Let us read John 5:24-29. "Truly, truly, I say to you, He who hears My word and believes Him who sent Me has eternal life, and does not come into judgment, but has passed out of death into life. Truly, truly, I say to you, An hour is coming, and it is now, when the dead will hear the voice of the Son of God, and those who hear will live. For just as the Father has life in Himself, so He gave to the Son to also have life in Himself; and He gave Him authority to execute judgment because He is the Son of Man. Do not marvel at this, for an hour is coming in which all in the tombs will hear His voice and will come forth: those who have done good, to the resurrection of life; and those who have practiced evil, to the resurrection of judgment."

Verse 24 says that as soon as a person believes, he has eternal life and will not come into judgment. He who hears the word of the Lord and believes the Father who sent the Lord has eternal life. But verse 29 says that those who have done good will come forth to the resurrection of life, while those that have practiced evil will come forth to the resurrection of judgment. The word *life* (Gk. *zoe*) in verse 29 is the same word as in verse 24. Those that have done good will come forth to the resurrection of *zoe,* and those that have done evil, to the resurrection of judgment. Verse 24 says clearly that we have eternal life already. But verse 29 says that some will not have eternal life until after the resurrection. Can you see the difference here?

Verse 25 is on the church age. It says that the dead will hear the voice of the Son of God. We all are these dead people. We have heard the voice of the Son of God, and as a result, we live. Verses 28-29 say, "Do not marvel at this, for an hour is coming in which all in the tombs will hear His voice and will come forth." Verse 25 says that an hour is coming and it is now. Verse 28, however, omits the phrase "and it is now," saying only that an hour is coming. Hence, it refers to the future, not to the present. Also, the Lord Jesus says that in the future all the ones from the tombs will come forth from the tombs. In verse 25, He refers to "the dead." In verse 28 He refers to the dead who are in the tombs. Verse 25 talks about the dead, referring to those dead in trespasses and sins. When the Lord speaks of those dead in the tombs, He is not referring to the death of the soul in sin; rather, He is referring to those dead in the body. All those who are dead in their body, that is, those who are in the tombs, will hear the voice of the Son of God for the second time. Those who have done good will go into the resurrection of life, and those who have done evil will go into the resurrection of judgment. This second time is the time when all those in the tombs will rise up.

Let us read Mark 10:30. "But that he shall receive a hundred times as much now at this time, houses and brothers and sisters and mothers and children and fields, with persecutions, and in the coming age, eternal life." Here the

Lord Jesus mentions eternal life again. We have to note what kind of eternal life this is. The eternal life in Mark 10:30 is not the eternal life of the church age spoken of in the Gospel of John or the eternal life in the new heaven and new earth. Please note that this eternal life is in the coming age. The phrase *the coming age* in the original language means the next age or the subsequent age. Today we are in the age of grace. The next age is the age of the kingdom, that is, the age of the millennium. Here, the Lord says that one can receive eternal life in the coming age. This does not refer to the eternal life we receive when we believe in the Lord.

Before the Lord spoke this word, a man came to Jesus asking what he should do to inherit eternal life. This was a question concerning works. Hence, the Lord Jesus told him of an eternal life that is gained by works. He told the young man that he must keep the law and sell all he had before he could inherit this eternal life. In the Gospel of John, the Lord Jesus shows us clearly that eternal life comes by grace and not by works. So why does He say here that we have to keep the law and sell all that we have, before we can inherit eternal life? It is because the eternal life described here in Mark 10 is different from the eternal life described in John. The eternal life in Mark 10 is received through works. The eternal life in John is received through faith.

After the young man left, the Lord Jesus looked around Him and said to the disciples, "How difficult it will be for those who have riches to enter into *the kingdom of God!*" (v. 23). In saying this, the Lord put eternal life and the kingdom together. After the Lord Jesus said this, the disciples wondered what His word meant. The Lord said, "Children, how difficult it is for those who trust in riches to enter into the kingdom of God! It is easier for a camel to pass through the eye of a needle than for a rich man to enter into the kingdom of God" (vv. 24-25). The disciples were astounded and asked who then could be saved. The Lord said that "with men it is impossible, but not with God, for all things are possible with God" (v. 27). Peter then asked what he would get for having left all to follow Him, and the Lord told them of the things that are to come. "Jesus said, Truly I say to you, There is no one who has left house or brothers or sisters or mother or father or children or fields for My sake and for the gospel's sake, but that he shall receive a hundred times as much now at this time, houses and brothers and sisters and mothers and children and fields, with persecutions, and in the coming age, eternal life" (vv. 29-30). They will receive eternal life in the kingdom.

Hence, the eternal life spoken of here is the eternal life in the kingdom. The eternal life in the kingdom is obtained through works. It is acquired through consecration, through suffering and bearing reproach for the Lord. For the Christian, the question of eternal life in this age is solved. The question of eternal life in eternity is also solved. But whether or not he will have eternal life in the kingdom depends on whether he loves the Lord, forsakes everything for the sake of the gospel, denies himself in everything, and rejects the world. It depends on whether or not he is living for money, for material gain, for his family, or for the worldly people. If he loves the Lord and forsakes all things for the sake of the gospel, the Lord promised that he will not lose these things even in this age, but on the contrary, he will gain a hundred times as much. If one gives up a little for the Lord today, he will reap a hundredfold return in the heavenly bank. Who can get such a high interest rate? A deposit of one dollar will yield a hundred dollars. You cannot find such a bank in the world. In addition, there is eternal life in the coming age.

In many places in Matthew, the phrase "eternal life" is used interchangeably with the word "kingdom." In these places the living ones are the ones who enter into the kingdom. For example, Matthew 7:14 says that the gate is narrow and the way is constricted that leads to life, and there are few that find it. Today many preach the gospel using this passage, and exhort people to enter the narrow gate and take the constricted way. But if one were saved through entering the narrow gate and taking the constricted way, salvation would not be of grace, but of works. Salvation would then become a reward for entering the narrow gate and taking the constricted way. The eternal life revealed in the book of Matthew does not refer to the eternal life of today; rather, it refers to the life in the millennial kingdom. In order to reign with Christ in the kingdom, a person must enter the narrow gate and take the constricted way. If one does not obey God's commandments and God's will, he will lose his eternal life. However, this does not mean that he will perish. But he will lose the eternal life in the kingdom.

If this problem is solved, then the problem of the ages in the Bible will be clearly resolved. In the age of the church, everything is by grace. At the end of the church age, God will establish His kingdom through His Son. In the kingdom only the faithful servants will reign with Christ by being resurrected from among the dead. The Bible shows us this very clearly.

PUNISHMENT IN THE MILLENNIAL KINGDOM

The Bible says that many children of God will have specific punishment. Many Christians have improper walks. They do not live in a godly way. They love the world and walk according to their will. They worship God according to man's way. They have not obeyed God's Word in taking care of God's work, but have instead done what they themselves like to do. They try to please men. They seek man's glory rather than God's glory and are not willing to stand in the same place of shame that the Lord stood in. They commit many mistakes and many sins. They have not been disciplined by God in this age. After they die and are resurrected on that day, can they reign with the Lord? The Bible says that we have to suffer and bear reproach with Him first before we can reign and be glorified with Him (2 Tim. 2:12). Not only have many believers never suffered, they have many sins. They love the world and walk according to the flesh. When they leave the world, they will still have much unrighteousness and many sins that were not dealt with. The Bible shows us that such believers will have specific and definite chastisement.

Matthew 18:23-35 speaks of a slave being forgiven of his debts by the master. Another slave owed this first one a debt. But the slave who was forgiven of his debt would not forgive his fellow slave. The first slave definitely represents a saved person, because he pleaded for the master's forgiveness, and the master, who was moved with compassion, released him and forgave his debt. We are all helpless persons coming to the Lord to seek grace. The Lord has forgiven our debt and has let us go. If this one represents a Christian, then whatever this one faces represents what we will face. The way the master deals with this slave will be the way the Lord deals with us.

Verses 28-30 say, "But that slave went out." He went out because he was now a free man. "But that slave went out and found one of his fellow slaves who owed him a hundred denarii, and he took hold of him and began to choke him, saying, Repay me what you owe. Then his fellow slave fell down and begged him, saying, Be patient with me and I will repay you. But he would not; instead, he went away and threw him into prison until he would repay what was owed." This passage is about one Christian not forgiving the sin of another. You are a forgiven person. But you are not willing to be forgiving. The Lord has forgiven you of ten thousand talents. Now your brother owes you a mere one hundred denarii, but you say in your heart that he must repay. He must repay you even the last cent. What will the result be then? Verses 31-33 continue, "Then his fellow slaves, seeing what had taken place, were greatly grieved and came and explained fully to their master all that had taken place. Then his master called him to him and said to him, Evil slave, all that debt I forgave you, because you begged me. Should you not also have had mercy on your fellow slave even as I had mercy on you?" That this person represents a saved one is again proved by the fact that the Lord had mercy on him. The Lord said, Should you not have mercy on your fellow slave as I have had mercy on you? Should you not forgive your fellow slave as I have forgiven you? This proves that this one represents one who has received God's mercy and forgiveness. He must be one that has life already. But he will not forgive other Christians. "And his master became angry and delivered him to the torturers until he would repay all that was owed" (v. 34). This one, who had been shown mercy and who had been forgiven, was put back into the hand of the torturers until he repaid all that was owed to the Lord.

Whether he could repay all that he owed is another matter. The fact is, he would have to suffer. This shows us that if a Christian will not forgive another, on that day the Lord will deal with him in the same way that he has dealt with others. If you would not forgive your brother, the Lord will deal with you according to your unforgiving attitude.

MERCY AND JUDGMENT

We know that our God is a righteous God. In the future, at the judgment seat, He will judge us according to righteousness. However, though there is righteousness at the judgment seat, there is mercy also. If you show mercy to others, the Lord will be merciful to you. If you are unforgiving toward others, and if you are so righteous and unyielding toward others' failures and weaknesses, the Lord will deal with you in righteousness in that day. If you are merciful to others, the Lord will show mercy to you. Luke 6:37 says that if you do not pass sentence on others, sentence will not be passed on you; if you will not judge others, you will not be judged, and if you forgive others, you will be forgiven. Some Christians are too mean today. When they criticize others they scrutinize every mistake others make. When they do their best to criticize and judge others, they have to be careful. In the future God will deal with them in the same way they deal with others. With what measure you measure to others, it will be measured to you. If you give to others good measure, pressed down, shaken together, and running over, the Lord will give to you in the same way. He who forgives will be forgiven, and to him who shows mercy, mercy will be shown.

Hence, the Bible says that mercy triumphs over judgment (James 2:13). There is one thing which even judgment cannot triumph over—a person showing mercy to others throughout his entire life. We cannot be without mistakes. But if we show mercy to others today, God will be unable to deal with us. Many Christians are not able to lose in their dealings with others. They argue all the time with others. They give little ground to others and grant themselves all the ground. But we should rather show mercy to others today. When the time of judgment comes, there will be some whom even the Lord of judgment will not be able to hold anything against. This does not mean that man can purposely change God's commandment. It simply means that if you are merciful to others while you are living on earth, God will be merciful to you. Your mercy today will triumph over your judgment tomorrow. The way you judge others will be the way that you will be judged. This grace is righteous. The way you treat others will be the way that the Lord will treat you. The way you treat others will fashion for you a vessel, with which God will measure out judgment to you. James 2:13 says, "For the judgment is without mercy to him who has shown no mercy; mercy triumphs over judgment." Those who show no mercy to others will be judged without mercy. But those who show mercy to others will triumph over judgment. Your mercy will surpass the judgment. This is an amazing fact.

Matthew 18 shows us clearly that God's children can still fall into the hand of the torturers. If they do, they will have to remain there until they pay off all their debts. Of course, there is no way to pay off all the debts. But at least one day they will learn to be merciful and to forgive others in the same way that the Lord showed mercy to them and forgave them. By then they will still have to show mercy to others. Hence, in verse 35 the Lord says, "So also will My heavenly Father do to you if each of you does not forgive his brother from your hearts." This portion of the Word is not spoken to unbelievers, but to Christians. It shows the relationship between the heavenly Father and His children and the relationship between the brothers.

Prior to this portion of the Word, Peter asked the Lord, "How often shall my brother sin against me and I forgive him? Up to seven times?" (Matt. 18:21). The Lord told him that he should forgive up to seventy times seven. Then the Lord spoke the word about the two slaves. Peter will face chastisement if he does not forgive his brother. The word of the Lord shows Peter that there is the possibility that he could be thrown to the torturers. There is the possibility that he could be put into prison. If there is the possibility for Peter to be thrown to the torturers and cast into prison, there is the possibility for us to be treated the same way also. That is why the Lord used the plural "you" in verse 35. His word is not for Peter only; it is for everyone. If we do not forgive each one of our brothers from our heart, the heavenly Father will do the same to us. Please remember that our eternal salvation in the new heaven and new earth is unshakable. Thank the Lord that this is by grace. But if our problems today are not dealt with specifically, we will still suffer specific punishment in the future kingdom.

Chapter Twenty-Four

HOW GOD DEALS
WITH THE BELIEVERS' SINS—
THE GEHENNA OF FIRE IN THE KINGDOM

There are many places in the Bible that mention God's punishment for the defeated Christians in the millennial kingdom. We will take a look at these places now. Later, we will draw a conclusion concerning them.

THE ENTRANCE INTO AND
THE POSITION IN THE KINGDOM

Let us first consider Matthew 18:1-3. "In that hour the disciples came to Jesus, saying, Who then is greatest in the kingdom of the heavens? And He called a little child to Him and stood him in their midst and said, Truly I say to you, Unless you turn and become like little children, you shall by no means enter into the kingdom of the heavens." Here the disciples asked a question concerning the kingdom of the heavens. It is a question concerning greatness in the kingdom. It is not a question concerning salvation and perdition, but a question concerning being great or small, high or low, in the kingdom. The Lord Jesus showed us that unless we turn and become like little children, we cannot enter into the kingdom of the heavens. Following this, verse 4 says, "He therefore who will humble himself like this little child, he is the greatest in the kingdom of the heavens." Verse 3 gives us the condition for entering the kingdom, while verse 4 gives us the way to be great in the kingdom. Verse 3 says that we must turn and become like children before we can enter the kingdom, and verse 4 says that if we continue to be children and humble ourselves, we will be the greatest in the kingdom of the heavens. This shows us that in the kingdom we should continue in the same way that we begin. The direction we face when we enter the kingdom should be the same direction we face when we continue in it. To enter into the kingdom of the heavens, we must turn and become like little children; and to be great in the kingdom of the heavens, we must continue to be humble like children. Here the Lord continues to bring up the matter of being like children.

Following this, the Lord said, "And whoever receives one such little child because of My name, receives Me" (v. 5). Whoever receives someone like this child because of Christ's name, that is, someone who turns to become like a child and who continues to be humble like a child, receives Christ. "And whoever stumbles one of these little ones who believe in Me, it is more profitable for him that a great millstone be hung around his neck and he be drowned in the open sea" (v. 6). This word indicates that stumbling others is a bigger problem than suffering and being killed in an ignoble way. Suppose someone kills you and casts your body into the sea. You are not even buried properly. Indeed this would be an unfortunate tragedy. But if you stumble others, your fate will be worse than this. Verse 7 says, "Woe to the world because of stumbling blocks! For it is necessary for stumbling blocks to come, but woe to that man through whom the stumbling block comes."

THE GEHENNA OF FIRE IN THE KINGDOM

Verses 1 through 7 are the general words of the Lord. We will just mention them briefly. We want to pay more attention to the words beginning in verse 8. The Lord Jesus expanded on this matter to point out that it is not only wrong to stumble others, but it is a serious and grave matter even to stumble yourself. Verse 8 says, "If your hand or your foot stumbles you, cut it off and cast it from you." Who does "you" refer to here? In verses 3 through 7, "you" refers to the disciples who asked the question in verse 1. After the Lord Jesus answered them, He told them to be watchful and not to stumble others. The Lord's words in verse 8 are directed at the same people. If a hand or a foot stumbles you, it is better to cut it off and cast it away. Of course, this need not be taken literally. If your hands steal and your feet walk in improper paths, that is, if there is sin and lust in you, you must deal with them. "It is better for you to enter into life maimed or lame than to have two hands or two feet and be cast into the eternal fire" (v. 8).

The Lord shows us that if Christians tolerate sin, they will suffer either the casting into the eternal fire with both hands and both feet, or the entering into life with one hand or one foot. This shows us clearly that there are those who deal with their sins and lusts in this age and who will enter into the kingdom with one hand or one foot. There are also those who will leave their lusts unchecked and will be cast into the eternal fire. The fire is an eternal fire, but it does not say that they will remain in the eternal fire forever. What the Lord Jesus did not say is as significant as what He did say. If a person has become a Christian but his hands or feet sin all the time, he will suffer the punishment of the eternal fire in the kingdom of the heavens. He will not suffer this punishment eternally, but will suffer it only in the age of the kingdom.

What does it mean to cut off a hand or a foot? When a man cuts off his hand or foot, he can still sin. If he does not have a foot, he can travel by car. If one of his hands is cut off, he can still sin with the other hand. It is not necessarily the Lord's intention that we cut off a hand or foot, for even if we do cut off a hand, we still cannot remove our lust. Therefore, this word must not refer to the outward body, but to the inward lust. What we have to cut off is that which drives us to sin.

Another thing that we have to realize is that the person spoken of here must be a Christian, for only a Christian is clean in his body as a whole and can thus enter into life after dealing with his lust in a single member of his body. It would not be enough for the unbelievers to cut off a hand or a foot. Even if they were to cut off both hands and both feet, they would still have to go to hell. In order to enter the kingdom of the heavens, it is better for a Christian to have an incomplete body than to go into eternal fire because of incomplete dealing.

Following this, verse 9 says, "And if your eye stumbles you, pluck it out and cast it from you; it is better for you to enter into life with one eye than to have two eyes and be cast into the Gehenna of fire." This shows us that if a saved person does not deal with his lust, he will not be able to enter into life, but will go into eternal fire. The eternal fire here is the Gehenna of fire. The Bible shows us that a Christian has the possibility of suffering the Gehenna of fire. Although he can suffer the Gehenna of fire, he cannot suffer it forever. He can only suffer it during the age of the kingdom.

Matthew 18 is not the only portion of Scripture that says this. Other portions of the Bible also contain the same teaching. For example, the Sermon on the Mount in Matthew 5—7 contains clear words of the same kind. Matthew 5:21-22 says, "You have heard that it was said to the ancients, 'You shall not murder, and whoever murders shall be liable to the judgment.' But I say to you that every one who is angry with his brother shall be liable to the judgment. And whoever says to his brother, Raca, shall be liable to the judgment of the Sanhedrin; and whoever says, Moreh, shall be liable to the Gehenna of fire." At the beginning of chapter five, we read that the Lord Jesus saw the multitude. But He did not teach the multitude; rather, He taught the disciples (v. 1). The Sermon on the Mount is for the disciples. Therefore, the one who reviles others in verse 22 is a brother. He calls another brother Raca, that is, good-for-nothing, or Moreh, that is, a fool. When he calls his brother this way, he shall be liable to the Gehenna of fire. This does not refer to an unsaved person, for an unsaved person will go to hell even if he does not call anyone Moreh. Every time the Bible talks about works, it refers to one who belongs to God. If such a one does not belong to God, there is no need to mention such things. This is a saved person, a brother, but because he has reviled his brother, he is liable to the Gehenna of fire.

Verse 23 says, "Therefore if you are offering your gift at the altar and there you remember that your brother has something against you." Many times others hold things against us on purpose, and there is nothing that we can do about it; but if others complain because of our reviling, we have to be careful when we offer up our gift at the altar. If you think poorly of a brother and have spoken something against him, you have to go to him and deal with the matter. "Leave your gift there before the altar, and first go and be reconciled to your brother, and then come and offer your gift" (v. 24). The important thing is to be reconciled to your brother. Verse 25 says, "Be well disposed quickly toward your opponent at law, while you are with him on the way." Your brother is the plaintiff, and you are the defendant. Now he is bringing you to court: "Lest the opponent deliver you to the judge, and the judge to the officer, and you be thrown into prison." Such a thing will happen in the kingdom. The kingdom is very strict.

Tonight I will speak a few frank and serious words. No two brothers or two sisters who are at odds with each other can appear in the kingdom together. In the coming kingdom, there will only be love and mercy; only those who love and show mercy to one another can be in the kingdom of the heavens. If I am involved in an argument with a brother, and if the matter is not dealt with in this age, then in the future, either both of us will be barred from the kingdom, or only one of us will get in. It cannot be that both of us will enter in. It is not possible for us to have a problem with each other and yet reign at the same time in the millennium in the future. In the kingdom all the believers are in one accord. There are absolutely no barriers between any two persons. If while we are on earth today, we have some friction with any brother or sister, or if we cause a hindrance to any brother or sister, we have to be careful. Either we will go in and the other will be excluded, or the other will go in and we will be excluded, or both will be excluded. The Lord says that while you are with him on the way you have to be reconciled to him. That means that while you and he are alive and before the Lord Jesus comes back, you have to be reconciled to him. The Lord Jesus will not tolerate two enemies complaining about each other in the kingdom. Today we may harbor complaints about others very easily; but these complaints will either keep us outside, keep others outside, or keep both us and others outside the kingdom. It seems that the church today is very free, but it will not be like this in that day. "While you are with him on the way," says the Lord. If you die, or if he dies, or if the Lord Jesus returns, the way is ended. Hence, you have to settle the matter quickly before the Lord comes back and while both he and you are on the way. "Lest the opponent deliver you to the judge." The judge is the Lord Jesus. "And the judge to the officer." The officer is the angel. "And you be thrown into prison." This shows us clearly that a brother who has offended another brother will suffer very severe punishment.

If you study this passage carefully, you will see that the prison here is the Gehenna of fire in verse 22, because verse 23 begins with "therefore." The words from verse 23 on are an explanation of the words in verse 22. Verse 22 says that anyone who calls his brother Moreh will be liable to the Gehenna of fire. Verses 23-25 follow by saying that those who are not reconciled to their brothers will be put into prison. Hence, the prison in verse 25 is very clearly the Gehenna of fire in verse 22. We are clear that there is no possibility for a Christian to perish eternally, but if a Christian has any unrepented of and unconfessed sins, which are not forgiven, he will suffer the Gehenna of fire. Notice the severity of the words of the Lord in verse 26: "Truly I say to you, You shall by no means come out from there until you pay the last quadrans." There is the possibility to come out if one has paid off everything. In the coming age, there is still the possibility of forgiveness, but one cannot come out until he pays the last quadrans and clears up everything with his brother.

Verses 27 through 30 form another section. This section is similar to the preceding one. "You have heard that it was said, 'You shall not commit adultery.' But I say to you that every one who looks at a woman in order to lust after her has already committed adultery with her in his heart." The commandment in the Old Testament says that we should not commit adultery, but the commandment of the New Testament says that we cannot even have adulterous thoughts. The word *woman* in the original language refers to another man's wife. If the woman is not another man's wife, there would be no possibility for adultery, because adultery is unfaithfulness in marriage. If this is not another man's wife, this cannot be considered adultery; it is fornication. The Bible judges fornication, but not as much as it judges adultery. Here it is saying that an adulterous thought is produced towards another's wife.

Second, the scope of the word in the original language for *look* here is not as broad as that of our word *look*. The word *look* brings too many under the category of this sin. In the original language it does not imply a casual looking but an intentional looking. Looking could simply be glancing at something accidentally on the street. *Watch* may be a better word because watching is an intentional looking. Furthermore, in the original language the watching here is done with a specific purpose. We could translate, "every one who watches a woman with the purpose of lusting after her." What the Lord condemns are not the sudden thoughts that enter your mind. What He is dealing with is the further watching for the purpose of lusting, after a sudden thought comes in. In other words, our sins do not lie in Satan's inciting of the flesh by giving us filthy thoughts. Our sins lie in the further watching after Satan has given us a sudden thought. This is adultery. Sudden thoughts are from Satan. Watching is from you. Sudden thoughts are temptations. Your watching is your accepting of the temptations. We must know how to differentiate between these two things.

Verse 29 says, "So if your right eye stumbles you, pluck it out and cast it from you." If your right eye causes you to watch, pluck it out and throw it away. "For it is more profitable for you that one of your members perish than for your whole body to be cast into Gehenna." If the lust is not removed, if the sin is not dealt with, a person will be "cast into Gehenna." Then verse 30 says, "And if your right hand stumbles you, cut it off and cast it from you, for it is more profitable for you that one of your members perish than for your whole body to pass away into Gehenna." These are words that the Lord Jesus spoke to the disciples. Christ told those

who belonged to Him and who desired that their righteousness
would excel that of the Pharisees and the scribes (v. 20) that
they have to deal with their sins. If they allow sin to develop
in them, though they will not eternally perish, there is the
possibility that they will "pass away into Gehenna." This is
what the Lord shows us in the book of Matthew.

FEARING HIM WHO HAS AUTHORITY
TO CAST INTO GEHENNA

Now let us look at what other places in the Bible say
concerning this matter. Luke 12:1 says, "Meanwhile, when
the myriads of the crowd were gathered together so that they
trampled on one another, He began to say to His disciples
first." He did not speak to everyone, but to the disciples first.
"Beware of the leaven of the Pharisees, which is hypocrisy."
The Lord's word proves that the disciples are not the
hypocrites; they are the Lord's people. Then in verses 4 and 5
the Lord said, "My friends, Do not fear those who kill the
body and afterward have nothing more that they can do. But
I will show you whom you should fear: fear Him who, after
killing, has authority to cast into Gehenna." The Word of God
is clear enough. It tells us, not once, but many times, that it
is possible for a Christian to be "cast into Gehenna." It says
this clearly here. The Lord told the disciples not to fear those
who kill the body but afterward can do nothing more. They
should not fear what some can do to their body, as long as
this is all they can do. But they should fear the One who can
cast them into Gehenna.

The verses following also prove that the ones spoken of
here are the disciples, that is, the believers. Verses 6 and 7
say, "Are not five sparrows sold for two assaria? And not one
of them is forgotten before God. But even the hairs of your
head have all been numbered. Do not be afraid; you are of
more value than many sparrows." Only Christians are
sparrows. The unsaved ones are not sparrows; they are crows.
In Matthew the lilies in the field refer to the Christians and
so do the sparrows. The sparrows neither sow nor reap nor
gather into barns (Matt. 6:26). This refers to Christians and
not to unbelievers. Here we are told clearly that it is possible

for God's "sparrows" to be "cast into Gehenna." Note also that it says the hairs of these ones have all been numbered. God would not exercise that much care on unbelievers. Therefore, what is meant here is that those belonging to the Lord need not fear what others do to their bodies. The One they must fear is God, for God has the authority to cast them "into Gehenna." We have to fear God who has the authority to deal with our souls. We have no fear of those who can only kill our bodies.

The next two verses, verses 8 and 9, are very precious. "Moreover, I tell you, Everyone who confesses in Me before men, the Son of Man will also confess in him before the angels of God; but he who denies Me before men will be denied before the angels of God." Christians can be divided into two classes: those who confess His name and those who do not. Some confess His name while others do not. Some are prepared to be persecuted while others are not. Some will only be Christians secretly. They desire man's glory. Others confess the Lord openly and are ready to be martyrs. Hence, you can see whom the Lord is talking about in these verses in Luke 12. We should not fear any suffering that comes through confessing His name. If we do not confess His name, our sin is more serious than all other sins. Consequently, He will not confess our names before the angels of God. When you take verses 1 through 9 together as a whole, you see that the "casting into Gehenna" in verse 5 is equivalent to the Lord not confessing their name before the angels in verse 9. The confessing before the angels can be illustrated by an example. Suppose a teenager has done something wrong and ends up in jail. His parents or other family members can bail him out of his trouble and let him slide by. But suppose that the child is really bad, and his parents feel that he needs some suffering. As a result, his parents will not bail him out. The same is true with the believers. Unless the Lord confesses our names, we will fall into punishment.

There is a wonderful word in Revelation 3:5. "He who overcomes will be clothed thus, in white garments, and I shall by no means erase his name out of the book of life, and I will confess his name before My Father and before His

angels." At the beginning of the kingdom, before the judgment
seat, the angels of God will take the Christians up to God.
The book of life will be there. In the book of life the names
of all the Christians are recorded. There will be many angels
and many Christians. The Lord Jesus will also be there. One
or more angels will then read off the names from the book
of life, and the Lord Jesus will confess some of the names.
Those whose names He confesses will then enter the kingdom.
When the names of the others are read, the Lord will not
say anything. In other words, He will not confess their names.
The angels will then put a mark against these names. Hence,
the overcomers' names are clean in the book of life, while the
defeated ones' names are marked. As for the unsaved ones,
their names do not appear in the book of life at all. One
group does not have their names in the book. Another group
has their names there, but their names are marked. And still
a third group, by the time of the kingdom, has their names
preserved in the same way as they were first written in the
book.

If your name is marked at the judgment seat, that does
not mean that you are through and are no longer saved.
Revelation 20:15 says, "And if anyone was not found written
in the book of life, he was cast into the lake of fire." This
shows us that those whose names are not recorded in the
book of life will be eternally in the lake of fire. Those whose
names do not appear in the book of life will be cast into the
lake of fire. This is at the beginning of the new heaven and
new earth. We cannot say that the ones in Revelation 3 do
not have their names written in the book of life. We can only
say that their names have been marked. By then they will
not be thrown into the lake of fire because their names are
already in the book of life. Eternal salvation is most secure;
it can never be shaken. But on the other hand, there is a
danger. If we tolerate sin, if we do not forgive others, if we
commit adultery, if we revile the brothers, if we are afraid
to suffer, to be ashamed, to be persecuted, and to confess the
Lord, we have to be careful, for God will cast us "into
Gehenna" so that we may be punished temporarily.

THE HURT OF THE SECOND DEATH

There are similar passages in the Bible that speak of these matters. Revelation 2:11 tells us that those who overcome will not be hurt by the second death, and Revelation 20:6 says that one group of people will not die again and that the second death will not have authority over them. The second death is the lake of fire at the end of Revelation 20. This means that the defeated ones *will* suffer the hurt of the second death. Although they will not suffer the second death itself, they will suffer the hurt of the second death. Once a person is saved, he will not suffer the second death. But this does not guarantee that he will not suffer the hurt of the second death.

We know that the time of the lake of fire and brimstone is the time when the new heaven and the new earth begins. Satan, the world, and death will all be cast into the lake of fire at that time (Rev. 20:10, 14). Also at that time a man will be cast into the lake of fire if his name is not recorded in the book of life. That will be the time when unbelievers are officially put into the lake of fire. However, during the millennium, the defeated Christians will suffer the hurt of the second death. Of course, this dealing will not be like the dealing that the unbelievers will have; it is not for eternity. If a Christian is joined to the world and if he loves the world and the things of the world, the Lord will allow him to go into corruption, to suffer a little of what the unbelievers will suffer. This is what being hurt by the second death in Revelation 2 means, and this word is spoken to Christians. The word "hurt" in the original language means to injure someone and to damage him. The second death will cause pain for some. From the time of the great white throne on, there is the second death itself, which is the suffering for eternity in the lake of fire and of brimstone. But in the millennium there is only the hurt of the second death. If some Christians have not dealt with their sins, they will still suffer the hurt and pain of the second death.

THE END BEING TO BE BURNED

Let us now read two passages from the book of Hebrews.

Hebrews 6:4-6 says, "For it is impossible for those who have once been enlightened and have tasted of the heavenly gift and have become partakers of the Holy Spirit and have tasted the good word of God and the powers of the age to come, and yet have fallen away, to renew themselves again unto repentance." These verses describe a person who has many qualifications. It is impossible for him to be an unsaved person. He has seen the light. He has seen the revealed God, the Only Begotten of the Father. He has known the love of God, and he has tasted the heavenly gift, the unique gift, Jesus Christ. In the Bible, *gifts* as a plural noun refer to the gifts of the Holy Spirit, and *gift* as a singular noun refers to the unique gift, the only begotten Son of God, as in John 3:16. This gift is different from the gifts of the Holy Spirit. This person not only has God and the Lord Jesus, but has also become a partaker of the Holy Spirit. He knows God, he has tasted the Lord Jesus, and he has the Holy Spirit living within him. Furthermore, he has tasted the good word of God and the powers of the coming age. The powers of the coming age are the powers of the millennial kingdom. The gifts and powers of the Holy Spirit are particularly abundant in the millennial kingdom. The millennial kingdom will be full of works of power, miracles, wonders, and other such things. To say that one has tasted the powers of the coming age is to say that one has tasted the things of the millennial kingdom. Hence, this person is definitely a saved person.

If such a person leaves the word of the beginning of Christ today and slips and falls, there is no repentance for him. He cannot start all over again to believe in the Lord Jesus. He has too much history with the Lord already. He has received so much rain. He has fallen and does not bring forth good things for God, but has brought forth thorns and thistles. He, like "the earth, which drinks the rain which often comes upon it and brings forth vegetation suitable to those for whose sake also it is cultivated, partakes of blessing from God. But if it brings forth thorns and thistles, it is disapproved and near a curse, whose end is to be burned" (vv. 7-8).

Notice three things about such a person and his end. First, he is disapproved. The word "disapproved" here is the same word as that used in 1 Corinthians 9:27 where Paul said that he feared that though he had preached the gospel to others, he himself would be rejected and would not be used by God anymore in this age and in the kingdom. To be disapproved, to be rejected, means that God will reject such a one and will not use him anymore in the kingdom. Second, such a person is "near a curse." The verse does not say that he will receive a curse, but the punishment that he receives is similar to a curse. He will not perish forever, but he will suffer the hurt of the second death and will suffer the Gehenna of fire in the kingdom. Third, his "end is to be burned." What is this? For example, a few weeks ago, I intended to burn up some land in Jen-ru. Could I burn the land forever? Could I burn the land for even five years? The burning here refers to something temporary.

Here it speaks about burning, whereas Matthew 5 says that some will be liable to the Gehenna of fire. If you put these two passages together, they match each other. If a Christian receives all these wonderful things but does not bear good fruit to God, but rather thorns and thistles, he will be burned. However this burning will only be for a while. Even an elementary school boy knows that if you burn a piece of land, the burning will stop after all the thorns are burned up. The burning in the kingdom will go on at most for a thousand years. How long it will actually burn depends on you. If you have brought forth many thorns and thistles, then there will be more burning. If you have brought forth few thorns and thistles, then there will be less burning.

How many things are there in us that are still not dealt with? How many things have not been cleansed away by the Lord's blood, and how many things are not yet confessed, dealt with, and settled with the brothers and sisters? These are the thorns and thistles referred to by the Lord. In Matthew 5 the Lord said that one cannot go out from there until every quadrans is paid. All the debts have to be paid. When everything is burned away, all the debts will be paid.

A Christian is likened to a field, and his improper behavior is likened to thorns and thistles. Suppose I have a five-acre piece of land. Is it possible that after it has been burned by fire, only two acres are left and three acres are gone? This is impossible. What is burned are the thorns and thistles. The field itself cannot be burned. In other words, only those things in Adam that are cursed, that should be removed but have not been removed, are to be burned. They are the object of the burning of the Gehenna of fire. The life that God has given us cannot be touched by fire. Therefore, after the thorns and thistles are burned away, the land will still remain. No part of it will be taken away. There is absolutely no problem with our salvation, but there is so much that has grown on top of it, so much that has come out of the flesh. If these things have not been dealt with by the blood of Jesus, we must pass through quite a bit of dealing.

Now let us look at another place, Hebrews 10:26-29. "For when we sin willfully after receiving the knowledge of the truth, there no longer remains a sacrifice of bulls and goats for sins, but a certain fearful expectation of judgment and fervor of fire, which is to consume the adversaries. Anyone who has set aside the law of Moses dies without compassion on the testimony of two or three witnesses. By how much do you think he will be thought worthy of worse punishment who has trampled underfoot the Son of God and has considered the blood of the covenant by which he was sanctified a common thing?" These verses refer to someone who has rejected Christ and returned to Judaism. He thinks that by spending a few dollars he can buy a bull or a goat as an offering for sin. But if someone has come to know Christ and returns to Judaism, he is trampling underfoot the Son of God and is regarding His blood as a common thing. He is treating the Lord like a bull or a goat. To him there is no difference between the Lord and a bull or a goat. The verse concludes, "And has insulted the Spirit of grace." While the Holy Spirit is giving him grace, he is insulting Him by going back to Judaism. These verses show us the way of an apostate. I will not say that such a one is saved; rather, I will only say that such a one may be saved. Perhaps he is not saved. The apostle does not tell us if such a one is saved or not. He only says that if a person has come to Christ and then returns to Judaism, he will suffer worse punishment.

His end is an expectation of judgment and fervor of fire. Here we see a kind of fire.

In addition to all of these passages, we also have the Lord's own words in John 15. Verse 2 says, "Every branch in Me that does not bear fruit, He takes it away; and every branch that bears fruit, He prunes it." These are not branches that have nothing to do with Him; these are branches in Him. What is indicated here may not refer to the temporary punishment, but to the discipline of this age. But look at verse 6: "If one does not abide in Me, he is cast out as a branch and is dried up; and they gather them and cast them into the fire, and they are burned." Some branches will be thrown into the fire and burned. Some branches have sprouted and have borne green leaves, but do not have fruit. Though they have life inwardly, they do not have fruit outwardly. The Lord Jesus said that they would be cast out, dried up, and burned in the fire. Here we see clearly that Christians may have to pass through the fire.

Having read all these passages, we can conclude that if a Christian does not take care of his sins properly, there will be punishment waiting for him. The Bible shows us clearly what kind of punishment this will be. It is not an ordinary kind of punishment but the punishment of the "Gehenna of fire." But it is the fire in the kingdom, not in eternity.

The question now is this: What kind of sin will bring us into this state? Once a person is saved, it is important that he deal with his sins. None of the sins that he has confessed, repented of, dealt with, and made recompense for under the blood of the Lord Jesus will come back to him at the judgment seat. All of these will be gone. Even the greatest sins will be gone. But there are many sins which will not be passed over. These are the sins that one regards in his heart. Psalm 66:18 says, "If I regard iniquity in my heart, / The Lord will not hear." What are the sins that the heart regards? The heart is where our love and desires lie. The heart represents our emotion. It represents the psychological man. If the heart regards iniquity, the Lord will not hear us. Many confessions are made only because the person knows that he has sinned. There is no hatred for the sin nor condemnation of the sin.

Such a one the Lord will not hear. Moreover, if we have a problem with another person that has not been solved, or if there are things that need to be forgiven but have not been forgiven, or if we have wronged others or the Lord, we have to deal with these things in a specific way. At the same time, we have to put these things under the Lord's blood. Only then will these things be dealt with, and we be delivered from the coming judgment.

SUMMARY

Now let us summarize what we have seen. The future of Christians is very simple. For a saved Christian the question of the new heaven and new earth, including all eternity, is solved. But the age of the kingdom is controversial. No one dares to say anything about what will happen. What we have to solve today is the problem of the kingdom. In the kingdom there are many ranks of Christians. Many will reign with Christ because they have worked faithfully and have undergone persecution, reproach, and suffering. Some may not have undergone persecution, reproach, and suffering, but they do not have sins either. They have lived a clean life. Although they have done nothing that deserves special merit, they have at least given a cup of water to a little one for the sake of the Lord's name (Matt. 10:42). They will also receive a reward, but their reward will be very small.

In the age of the kingdom, some Christians will receive a reward in the kingdom. Some will receive a great reward; others will receive a small reward.

Those who will not receive a reward are also divided into a few categories. One group will not enter into the kingdom at all. The Bible does not tell us where they will go. It only says that they will be kept outside the kingdom in the outer darkness (Matt. 8:12; 22:13; 25:30; Luke 13:28). They will be left outside the glory of God. Second, there will be many who, in addition to not having worked well, have specific sins not yet dealt with. They are saved, but when they die, they still have sins which they have not repented of and dealt with. They still have the problem of sin with them. These ones will be temporarily put into the fire. They will come out only after they have paid all their debts. This will last at most until the end of the kingdom. I do not know how long this period will actually be.

There are still many things which we are not clear about concerning the future, but the Bible has shown us enough. Although there are details which we have not yet seen, we do know what the children of God will face. Some will receive a reward; some will go into corruption. Some will be put into prison, and still some will be cast into the fire and be burned.

The matter of our salvation is quite clear. When a man trusts in the Lord Jesus, both salvation and eternal life are settled for him. But after a person is saved and up until he dies, his works, that is, his failures or his victories, will determine his fate in the kingdom. Our God is a just God. On the one hand, our salvation is free, and those who believe will have eternal life. No one can overturn this fact. On the other hand, we cannot sin at will just because we have received eternal life. If we bring forth thorns and thistles, we will be burned. If the Lord Jesus cannot disassociate us from our sins and if we have not settled everything in our lives, God has no choice but to chastise us in the future. He has no choice but to cleanse us with specific punishments, so that we can be together with Him in the new heaven and new earth. God is a just God. What He has prepared is also just. Once we have seen these things, we must learn the lesson and take the warnings from God.

THE PROPER ATTITUDE IN READING THE BIBLE

Concerning the way we study the Bible, I would like to mention a few things. First, there is a group of people who believe only in grace. Whenever they read about things related to the kingdom in the Bible, they apply it to the Jews. If you listen to their sermons and read their books, they invariably push everything related to the kingdom onto the Jews. Everything related to grace is for the church, and all the terrible things are for the Jews. To them, everything burdensome, difficult, and demanding is for the Jews, not for us. This is foolishness. God's Word is for His children, whether they are Jews or Gentiles. Some say that Paul never specifically said that his Epistles were written to Gentiles, and therefore, they are not for Gentiles. But this kind of explanation explains away and cuts apart the Word of God. Others say that the portions of the Scriptures quoted earlier refer to unbelievers only. But how can the distinction between overcomers and non-overcomers exist among the sinners? This is foolish talk. The Word of God shows us these matters in a clear and definite way. We have to eat what God has given us, whether it is sweet or bitter. When men hear about grace, they are happy; when they hear about the kingdom, they are unhappy. But the Word is balanced. On the one hand, we see grace; on the other hand, we see righteousness.

There is the fable of the eagle and the cat. Once a cat met an eagle. The eagle said to the cat, "The sky is really great. It has this and it has that. Would you like me to take you up to the sky?" The cat said, "No, I do not care to go there." When the eagle asked why not, the cat said, "There are no mice in the sky. If there were mice there, I would go. But since there aren't, I won't." Heaven is so holy; sin, the world, and Satan are not there. If God brings you to heaven, will you be able to live there? If we do not turn today, we will have to wait until we are worthy to enter in. It is true that the Lord Jesus has saved us, but subjectively speaking, if we do not allow the Holy Spirit to work the Lord Jesus into us, God will have to chastise us that we may receive the benefit and be counted worthy to be with Him. If we only preach grace without preaching the kingdom, the church will suffer and God's children will suffer; and when the kingdom comes, there will be even greater suffering. I must speak as I ought to speak.

I admit that after my speaking in these few days, some will increase their opposition against me. If these are my words, I am willing to see them opposed. Even I myself would oppose them. But if these things are the Word of God, and if God has spoken them, what can I do? How I wish that I did not have to talk about these things. How I wish that I could preach something that everyone would like to hear. I am not Matthew. I am not Mark. I am not Paul. I did not write the book of Hebrews, and I did not write Revelation. If I were the writer, I could change things. But these things are God's Word. God has spoken them and determined that they should be so. My friends, when you read the Bible, you have to read what God has said. You must not consider what man has said. You should only care for what God has said.

The greatest difficulty today in studying the Bible lies in the prejudice in the mind of God's children. They have what they consider as truth and what they consider as heresy. They think that everything that matches them is truth, and everything that does not match them and that differs from them is heresy. Regardless of how scriptural a basis there is for it, any thought or concept contrary to theirs is considered heresy. But if that is one's attitude, he is through. At issue today is what God has said.

I am happy in my heart because I can preach the "heresy" of God's Word and I can oppose the "truth" in man's teaching. Today we have to be clear before the Lord. We cannot be under any other authority but that of God's Word. I know no other authority. I do not know what theology is; I do not know what man's word is; I do not know what the tradition of the church is. I only know what the Bible says, and only what it says counts. We must subject ourselves to it only. We cannot change God's Word. The Word of God tells us the destiny of His children. It tells us what we will experience in the kingdom. We must pay attention to these issues because sooner or later we will face them again. If we pay attention to them we will be careful how we live on earth today.

The second thing that we must realize is that only those who understand the truth can oppose heresy. One heresy cannot oppose another heresy. But all heresies are not pure heresy; they are the truth plus a little error. Heresy is to add wrong things to right things. Add a little of man's thought to God's thought, and you will have heresy.

Because Catholicism does not fully know the truth in the Bible, it preaches the doctrine of purgatory. If you do not know the truth that we have released in the last few meetings, you will not be able to tell whether the doctrine of purgatory is right or wrong. Now that you have heard these messages, you will realize that the doctrine of purgatory is absolutely

462 THE GOSPEL OF GOD

wrong. You can say that it is heresy. In the Bible we see that God's discipline of the Christians happens in the millennium, but Catholics say that there is a purging going on today. They say that if a Christian does not live up to standard on earth today, he will not be able to go to heaven. Hence, he must be purged. Therefore, they say that as soon as a Christian dies, he begins to be purged and is purged until the job is done. However, there is absolutely no such teaching in the Bible. The Bible never says that as soon as a Christian dies, he will be purged in Hades. The Bible shows us that there will be the discipline in the kingdom in the future, but there is no purging in Hades today.

Second, Catholics make another grave mistake. They think that if they secure for themselves indulgences while they are alive or if the priests pray for them after they die, they will be relieved of some of the purging of purgatory. But the Bible never says anything like this. The Bible says only that he who has mercy on others will obtain mercy. Praying by the priest will not do anything for the dead. The Bible never teaches us to pray for the dead.

Third, Catholics tell people that a man will not be saved until he has been completely purged in purgatory. This is an absolute overturning of the teaching of the Bible. The Bible shows us that there is no other name in heaven or on earth besides that of the Lord Jesus whereby we must be saved (Acts 4:12). Only He can save us. Apart from the Lord Jesus, there is no salvation. Discipline and chastisement are not for salvation but for sanctification. The matter of our salvation is settled long before God disciplines us, but there are still things in us that do not match Him. There are still imperfections and areas that are not up to standard. There- fore, there is the discipline in this age and the discipline in the coming kingdom.

Once a person is clear about the biblical truth, he will see the heresy in Roman Catholicism. The Roman Catholic Church takes a few verses and utilizes them for her own purpose. But if we know the biblical truth, we will realize that the doctrine of purgatory annuls grace. Thank God that, although I am a filthy sinner, through the Lord Jesus I am now saved. When I die, I do not have to be purged any further, because salvation is not of me, but of the Lord Jesus. Surely I am saved. Now we know what discipline is. Discipline is God's means to make us perfect as He is perfect. He chastises us so that we will be like Him, even the same as He is. This has nothing to do with our salvation. It is a matter within His family.

Finally, only after we know this will we be able to deal with the heresy in Protestantism. Today among the Protestants, two kinds of errors are being promulgated. First, one group of Protestant theologians proposes that since a man is "once saved, always saved," he can get away with anything in his conduct. Since a Christian is saved eternally, they say, he could be evil until the day he dies and still be in the kingdom. He would, however, occupy a lower position in the kingdom. His greatest loss is confined to occupying a lower position in the kingdom. This kind of teaching will make a man loose and irresponsible. What then is grace to them? To them grace is an excuse for looseness and licentiousness.

There is another group of Protestants who say that after a man believes, there is still the possibility that he will not be saved. Perhaps he can be saved and unsaved again three or four times within a day. If that were the case, the book of life would get very messy indeed. A brother once said that if we are not eternally saved once we have believed, then the book of life will be extremely thick. My name alone would be deleted and inserted many, many times. If a man is condemned as soon as he sins and if he is bound for hell as soon as he transgresses, we must wonder whether salvation is by grace or by works.

Both of these groups are too extreme, even though both have their scriptural basis. The Bible shows us clearly that when a man is saved, he is eternally saved. The Bible also shows us clearly that it is possible for a Christian to be "cast into Gehenna" temporarily. But the problem is that some brothers hold onto one side, insisting that salvation is eternal and that there is no such thing as discipline in the kingdom, while other brothers hold onto the other side, insisting that if we can be "cast into Gehenna," eternal life is shaky, and therefore we can go into eternal perdition. But if we see the difference between the age of the kingdom and the eternal age and the difference between the temporary punishment of the millennium and eternal punishment, we will be clear that a Christian can receive punishment in the future, but at the same time, God has given His sheep eternal life, and they can never lose it. This knowledge gives us the boldness to say that once we are saved, we are eternally saved. After a man has been saved by grace, he will never perish again. Thus, not only have we properly settled the problem of the purgatory of Catholicism, but we have also made a clear distinction between eternal salvation and discipline. May the Lord grant us grace tonight and show us that the matter of eternal salvation is solved because of the work of Jesus of Nazareth, but as for one's situation in the kingdom, it is determined by the person himself.

CHAPTER TWENTY-FIVE

HOW GOD DEALS WITH THE BELIEVERS' SINS— CLEANSING AND CONFESSION

After a man has believed in the Lord Jesus, all his past sins are forgiven by the redemptive work of the Lord. But what should he do if he sins again after he has believed and is saved? It is not right to sin, but sinning is a fact of life. It is a shame for a Christian to sin, but it is also an undeniable fact that Christians do sin. We know that we should not fail and that we should not make mistakes, but we have to admit that we do have times of failure and we do make mistakes. What then will we do with these sins? To put it more accurately, what will God do with these sins? Earlier we mentioned temporary chastisement. God warns us that if we become apostate, we will be punished in the millennial kingdom. But if we want to deal with our sins and if we want to be cleansed of our sins, what should we do? How can our sins be washed away and forgiven? Although there are only three or four places in the whole Bible that mention this problem, they afford us clear light. In order to know how to deal with this problem, all we have to do is to read these few passages.

ONE CLEANSING BY THE BLOOD

Tonight let us start from the beginning. We know that when the Lord Jesus was crucified on the cross, He shed His blood to wash away all of our sins. After He washed away our sins, He sat down at the right hand of God (Heb. 1:3). If, after we are saved and have been cleansed of our sins, we sin again and are defiled again, will the blood of the Lord

Jesus wash away our sins again? Man thinks that if he sins, the blood of the Lord Jesus will have to cleanse away his sins again. But there is no such truth in the Bible. The blood cleanses away our sins only once; it never cleanses twice. There is no such thing as a re-cleansing of man's sins.

The book of Hebrews shows us clearly that there is only one cleansing of sin. Hebrews 10:1-14 says, "For the law, having a shadow of the good things to come, not the image itself of the things, can never by the same sacrifices year by year, which they offer continually, perfect those who draw near. Otherwise would they not have ceased to be offered, because those worshipping, having once been purified, would have no longer had the consciousness of sins? But in those sacrifices there is a bringing to mind of sins year by year. For it is impossible for the blood of bulls and goats to take away sins. Therefore, coming into the world, He says, 'Sacrifice and offering You did not desire, but a body You have prepared for Me. In burnt offerings and sacrifices for sin You did not delight. Then I said, Behold, I have come (in the roll of the book it is written concerning Me) to do Your will, O God.' Saying above, 'Sacrifice and offerings and burnt offerings and sacrifices for sin You did not desire nor delight in' (which are offered according to the law), He then has said, 'Behold, I have come to do Your will.' He takes away the first that He may establish the second, by which will we have been sanctified through the offering of the body of Jesus Christ once for all. And every priest stands daily, ministering and offering often the same sacrifices, which can never remove sins; but this One, having offered one sacrifice for sins, sat down forever on the right hand of God, henceforth waiting until His enemies are made the footstool for His feet. For by one offering He has perfected forever those who are being sanctified."

We see that the Lord Jesus has offered Himself up once as a sin offering for our sins. He has accomplished eternal redemption once for all. By His one work we are eternally perfected. Verse 2 implies that those who have been purified no longer have the consciousness of sins. Hence, there is only one offering of the Lord Jesus. There is no second offering.

If someone rejects this sin offering, there will be no other sin offering for him. This is why verse 26 says that if we sin willfully, there is no more sacrifice for sins. The sins of a sinner are forgiven through the cross of the Lord Jesus. After a Christian is saved, even if he sins, the Lord Jesus cannot die for his sins again. His one-time accomplishment has accomplished everything eternally. In Him everything is included.

Let us now read a few verses from chapter nine. Verses 25, 26, and 28 say, "Nor in order that He might offer Himself often, just as the high priest enters into the Holy of Holies year by year by the blood of other creatures; since then He would have had to suffer often since the foundation of the world. But now once at the consummation of the ages He has been manifested for the putting away of sin through the sacrifice of Himself....So Christ also, having been offered once to bear the sins of many, will appear a second time to those who eagerly await Him, apart from sin, unto salvation." His coming the second time will have nothing to do with their sins; rather, it will be for their salvation. Verses 12 through 14 say, "Not through the blood of goats and calves but through His own blood, entered once for all into the Holy of Holies, obtaining an eternal redemption. For if the blood of goats and bulls and the ashes of a heifer sprinkling those who are defiled sanctifies to the purity of the flesh, how much more will the blood of Christ, who through the eternal Spirit offered Himself without blemish to God, purify our conscience from dead works to serve the living God?" Verse 9, speaking of the first tabernacle, says that it is "a figure for the present time." According to this tabernacle "both gifts and sacrifices are offered, which are unable to perfect, according to conscience, him who worships."

By reading chapters nine and ten we see that those in the Old Testament differ from those in the New. If I were in the Old Testament and committed a sin, I would have only one way to deal with my sin. If I had enough money, I would buy a bull. If I did not have that much money, I would buy a goat. If I could not afford either, I would buy a turtledove. Then I would ask a priest to offer up the sacrifice for me to atone my sin. When I saw the bull or goat, I would be happy at heart, for I would know that the offering had served as a substitute for my punishment. Because the blood of the bull or goat would be like my blood, God would forgive me. I could go home happy and joyful at heart. I would be the happiest person on earth, because my sins would have been forgiven. I did not have my sins anymore. The darkness in my conscience would be removed, and I would suffer no more. But after two days, I would begin to think, What if the sacrifice offered that day did not work? What if the priest did not do the right thing the other day? Because of these thoughts, I would begin to worry and suffer again. Finally, I would decide to buy another bull or goat, take it to the priest, and tell him that the sin offering the other day was not done well, and ask him if he would perform the offering once more. The priest then would slaughter the bull or goat and offer it once more to God, and assure me that the bull or goat had been offered up for my sins.

When the conscience was troubled in the Old Testament, one could always bring another bull or goat to offer a sin offering through the priest. This is what Hebrews 9 shows us. It tells us that the blood of bulls and goats did not do a complete job. Chapter ten says that if a complete job had been done, there would have no longer been consciousness of sins. God reckoned that the work of bulls and goats was incomplete according to the conscience, because every time a person's conscience lost its peace, he felt that his sins had not yet been fully taken care of, and there was the need for further offerings.

However, the apostle shows us that a Christian does not have to do the same thing. The propitiatory sacrifice that God has set up in the New Testament is not a bull or goat but His very own Son. When His Son came to the earth, He said plainly that God did not desire nor delight in bulls and goats. Instead, God prepared a body for Him that He might die to accomplish the work of eternal redemption. The Lord has accomplished on the cross the sacrifice for eternal redemption. Now we are able to obtain this eternal redemption. He has offered up a sacrifice of eternal redemption, thus accomplishing an eternal redemption. Because of this eternal redemption, we are eternally perfected. He is the Son of God. Because His eternal work has been accomplished once, we do not need to offer up sin offerings anymore. We cannot offer up a sin offering for the same sin any longer, for the Lord Jesus has accomplished all the work.

The Son of God cannot be crucified for our sins again. One cannot trample underfoot the blood of God's Son and make it something common. If something is one of a kind, it is precious. But if there are two of a kind, they are common. To treat the blood of the Son as common means to consider it the same as the blood of bulls and goats. But if you honor His blood and consider it as something unique, it will be precious to you. Here is the sin offering which He has accomplished. After the Lord has accomplished this work, God said that there cannot be any other work. The Son of God cannot die again. His work is finished. If you want it, you have to trust Him for it. You cannot add anything to it. Either you depend on Him or you have nothing. After a man has been enlightened by the truth, there is no more sacrifice for sins for him. There is only one sin offering. This is what we preach to others. Those who come to worship through this one sacrifice will have their consciences cleansed. They will no longer have the consciousness of sins. All their sins are washed away, and there is no more consciousness of sins. Furthermore, there is no need for another cleansing. The Bible never teaches the doctrine of a second cleansing. The blood of the Lord Jesus cannot cleanse us again. Once we have been cleansed, we are cleansed forever.

RECEIVING THE CONTINUAL CLEANSING
AFTER WE HAVE BELIEVED

The question now is this: What should we do if we sin again? What should we do if we become filthy again? All the sins we committed before we were saved have been washed away by His blood. But what should we do about the sins that are committed after we are saved? We do not want to be chastised. We do not want to lose the kingdom. We do not want to suffer the hurt of the second death. What can we do before God? Let us consider 1 John 2:1: "My little children, these things I write to you that you may not sin." A Christian's goal is not to sin. John wrote these words so that we would not sin. According to the status that Christians possess, it is possible for us not to sin. Unfortunately, according to actual history, we often do sin. Positionally speaking, we should not sin. But experientially speaking, we often do sin. There is no need to sin. But sin is an unshakable fact.

John continues, "If anyone sins." Here we are dealing with the problem of a Christian who sins. He is a little one of God; he belongs to God. If he sins, what should he do? "We have an Advocate with the Father, Jesus Christ the Righteous." It does not say that we have an Advocate with God; rather, it says that we have an Advocate with the Father. Thus, this verse refers to the children of God. It refers to those that have been saved. If anyone among the saved ones, the children of God, sins, he has an Advocate with the Father. This is not a dispute in a law court, but a matter within a family.

The word *Advocate* in the original language is *paracletos*. *Para* means alongside of. To be alongside of means that you are there and another is there. You are in Shanghai, and this one is also in Shanghai. When you go to Canton, this one also goes to Canton. It is like railway tracks. You cannot have one track in Szechwan and another in Nanking. *Cletos* means helper. A *paracletos,* therefore, is someone who is alongside helping. You can run away. But wherever you run, the *paracletos* will be there also. Many who help are very good, but they sometimes come too late. There may be a lot of rice in Shanghai, but the starving ones in Szechwan will not be able to get it, because it is not alongside. The Greeks used the word *paracletos* to refer to a defense lawyer in court. Suppose that you do not understand the law, and others accuse you. Others may sue you or take advantage of you. But you do not have a way to answer them. Now there is a *paracletos* to answer for you. Others charge that you have sinned. But your *paracletos* will say that you do not have sin. He will answer for you like a defense lawyer. The meaning here is to have someone next to you to speak for you. If a

Christian sins, there is One with the Father speaking for him.

Satan will never stop his accusations against the Christians. Revelation 12:10 tells us that he accuses the brothers day and night. Day and night we are the defendants and he is the accuser. But we have an Advocate, who is Jesus the Righteous. Here it says that He is the Advocate. Here He is not the gracious One, but the righteous One. Why does it not say that He is the gracious One? It is because in the heavenly law court there is no talk of grace, in the same way that there is no talk of grace in earthly law courts. Any judge who wants to forgive others is an unrighteous judge. Only those who are for righteousness can be judges. God is for righteousness. He did not forgive our sins unrighteously. He did not overlook our sins, gloss over our sins, or let us get by with our sins. Rather, He judged our sins in righteousness.

The Lord Jesus does not defend us by saying that the temptation was too great and as little children we could not handle it, and that therefore God has to grant us grace. The Lord Jesus does not say that Christians are too small and their knowledge is too little, that the flesh is too weak and the enticement of the world is too strong. He does not say that the wiles of Satan are too cunning and that there is no way to reject Satan. This is not the way that the Lord Jesus makes our defense. He does not plead for grace. Neither is He there as a dispenser of grace. John says that Jesus Christ is the Righteous. He tells God that on account of Him and what He has done, God has to forgive us.

How does this Advocate make a defense for us? We are told in the next verse: "And He Himself is the propitiation for our sins, and not for ours only but also for those of the whole world" (1 John 2:2). The Lord Jesus makes His defense for us based on His accomplished work, that is, His propitiation on the cross for us. As a result, we are able to come to God. This is a complete propitiatory sacrifice. It includes all the sins of all the Christians in time and space. When this propitiatory sacrifice is shown to God, God no longer has a reason to punish the Christians. The Lord's propitiatory sacrifice is not just for past sins, but for all present and future sins as well. The verb in this verse is in the present tense, not in the past tense. God cannot condemn us based on Satan's accusation, because Christ's redemptive work accomplished on the cross includes all the sins of today and all the sins that will be committed until the day of His return. All our sins are included in His work. God must forgive us. He cannot do otherwise, because this forgiveness has a foundation.

THE LORD JESUS AS ADVOCATE FOR CHRISTIANS

The work of the Lord Jesus as Savior is for sinners. The work of the Lord Jesus as Advocate is for Christians. As the Savior, the Lord Jesus accomplished the work of the cross. As the Advocate, the Lord Jesus applies the work of the cross. The sins of sinners are forgiven through the redemption of the cross. The sins of Christians are forgiven through the advocacy that is based upon the redemption of the cross. This advocacy presents the work of the cross to God. It shows God what the Lord Jesus has done, so that God cannot punish man for his sins. We have an Advocate before God. His death is presented to God.

The Lord Jesus has become an Advocate for every Christian who sins, in the same way that He has become the Savior for every sinner. It is not that first we repent, believe, and are regenerated, and then the Lord Jesus dies for us. Rather, it was while we were yet sinners that Christ became our Savior (Rom. 5:8). In the same way, it is not that we first repent, and then He becomes our Advocate. Rather, even while we are sinning, He becomes our Advocate. It is not that He becomes our Advocate when we confess our sins before God. Rather, even while we are sinning, He becomes our Advocate. This is why John says that if any man sins, we have an Advocate with the Father. He does not say that first we repent, confess our sins, and pray for forgiveness, and then He becomes our Advocate. Instead, John says that if anyone sins, we have an Advocate with the Father already. Whenever you sin, at that moment the Lord Jesus is already your Advocate before God. At that very moment, the Lord Jesus will show God His work of the cross, and God will have to let your sins go. A Christian can confess and repent because the Lord Jesus is his Advocate. Because we have the Lord Jesus as our Advocate, advocating and speaking for us while we sin, we eventually repent, confess our sins, and ask for forgiveness. The Lord Jesus' work of advocacy does not happen at the moment we repent. Rather, it happens while we are sinning. When we sin, the Lord Jesus is our Advocate already. Afterwards, we are brought to repentance and confession. The Lord Jesus accomplished all the work in one day. Everything is included in that work. Today the Lord can present this work to God. God can no longer punish us, because all the debts have been paid. All the debts, past and future, are paid. All our sins have been washed away by the blood of Jesus.

WALKING IN THE LIGHT AS HE IS IN THE LIGHT

He is the Advocate. But what should we do on our part? Let us now go to 1 John 1:7. "But if we walk in the light as He is in the light, we have fellowship with one another, and the blood of Jesus His Son cleanses us from every sin." What does it mean to be in the light? Man thinks that to be sinless and to be holy is to be in the light. But that is not the sense here. John does not say that we should walk in the light as God *walks* in the light. It is not said of God here that He *walks*. If that had been said, the meaning would be entirely different. It says here that we should walk in the light as He *is* in the light.

What is the meaning of this difference? For example, in this meeting hall there are many light bulbs, but we call them the light. We are now sitting in the light. On the other hand, while we are meeting, many people often sit on the stairs next door. They are in darkness. They may not have sinned out there. They may not have stolen from others out there. Perhaps they are even better and holier than we. But those who sit in the light can see, while those who sit in darkness cannot see. For God to be in the light means that God can now be seen.

In the Old Testament, God was shrouded in darkness. He was in the Holy of Holies, and man could not see Him. In the Holy Place there was a lamp, and in the outer court there was the sun, but in the Holy of Holies, there was no light at all. God was an unknown God there. Man could only make conjectures about Him. But thank the Lord that today God has been manifested in Jesus of Nazareth. God is now in the light; He is no longer in darkness. Today God is a known God, a revealed God. When you see God today, you know that He is God. The gospel concerning Jesus of Nazareth is the revelation of God. The shining out of the light of the gospel is the shining out of God. When the light of the gospel shines out, we see God. I am not saying that we should not be holy or that we should not reject sin. I am saying that this verse tells us that as God is in the light, we should therefore walk in the light. As God has manifested Himself in the light of the gospel, even so we should see God in the light of the gospel. We no longer look for God in the Old Testament. Today God has manifested Himself. If He had not manifested Himself, we would be hopeless. If He had not manifested Himself, we would still be bewildered, not knowing what kind of God He is. We would still have to make conjectures about Him. Thank God that He has been manifested. Today our God is no longer a "backstage" God. He is now the "onstage" God, the revealed God. The word *revelation* is *apocalypsis* in Greek. *Apo* means away, and *calypsis* means veil. Hence, *apocalypsis* means the taking away of a veil. I used to watch theater performances. Onstage there is always a thick curtain. You do not know what is behind the curtain. An *apocalypsis* is the opening up of the curtain.

Today God is in the light. He is an open God. What then should we do? We should walk in the light. This means we will see God and know God in the light. Today we do not know God by way of conjecture as those in the Old Testament did. Today God has spoken. There is no need to make conjectures anymore. Today God is already in the light. He has already revealed Himself in the gospel. If we walk in this revelation, the result is fellowship. There will be fellowship between Christians, and there will be fellowship with God.

Since we are participants in the gospel and since God is

also a participant in the gospel, the blood of His Son Jesus cleanses us from all sin. If we truly know God in the gospel, we will see that the blood of His Son Jesus is continually and eternally cleansing us of all sin (1 John 1:9). In the original language, this verse says that the blood of Jesus His Son is continually cleansing us from all sin. The Bible never shows us that the blood of the Lord Jesus does a second cleansing work. It shows us that the blood of Jesus cleanses us all the time. There are no multiple cleansings. There is only the continual cleansing. The Bible never has the thought of multiple cleansings. The biblical truth is a continual cleansing.

The blood of the Son of God continually cleansing us from our sins is the work of the Advocate. The work of the cross is once for all. But the operation of His cleansing and His blood is continuous. The cross dealt with our sins and washed away our sins only once. But it is forever effective. Why is it forever effective? Why is it cleansing us continually? It is because His Son is presenting the accomplished work to God continually. It is not a re-cleansing, but a continual demonstration to God that He has died and that all the sins are dealt with already. Today He is continually cleansing away all of our sins. All our sins are included here. The effectiveness of His blood lasts forever because the Lord Jesus is our Advocate continually in heaven. His work as the Advocate is a continuation and extension of His work as the Savior. The work of the Savior happened only once, but it is continued in the work of the Advocate. This is God's side of the work.

FORGIVENESS THROUGH CONFESSION

We must never neglect God's side. However, we must never forget our side either. It is true that the Lord Jesus is presenting His blood and His accomplished work before God continually. But if we sin intentionally, continuously, and without repentance, repudiation, or an inclination to deal with our sins, the work of the Lord's blood will lose its effect and efficaciousness for us. The work of the Lord's crucifixion is not just for us, but for the whole world also. The one work of the Lord Jesus has included everyone. But this work of

the Lord can be realized only in those who believe in Him.
Christ's work of advocacy is the same in principle. It is
continuous. Regardless of whether a Christian will confess
and repent of his sins or not, the cleansing work of Christ
is continually effective. But how this can be realized in the
believers is another problem.

First John 1:7 tells us that a Christian is forgiven of his
sins before God because of the work of Christ. On the other
hand, verse 9 shows us what we should do on our side. "If
we confess our sins, He is faithful and righteous to forgive
us our sins and cleanse us from all unrighteousness." First
John 2:1 tells us that the Lord Jesus is our Advocate. But
1 John 1:9 tells us that on our side we have to confess our
sins. This does not mean that it is our confession that grants
us forgiveness. If confession itself can earn forgiveness, the
forgiveness is unrighteous. Suppose that I stole a hundred
dollars from a brother, and I go to him and confess my sin.
If he forgives me on account of that confession, is he
righteous? If that were the case, I could steal another hundred
dollars again and could confess again. If confession alone can
earn us forgiveness, this is the most unrighteous thing there
is. If that were the case, we could not say that God is faithful
and righteous. We would have to say that God is an unrighteous, sloppy God, who overlooks our sins.

Why does John say that God is righteous to forgive? It is
because the Lord Jesus has become our Advocate. His blood
has cleansed away all of our sins. Our sins have been judged
and condemned in Christ. Therefore, when we confess our
sins, God is faithful and righteous to forgive us. If I have
stolen money from a brother and someone has paid it back
for me, then confession will indeed bring me forgiveness.
Without the blood of the Son of God, God's forgiveness would
be unrighteous. Today the blood of the Son of God has been
shed. The Son of God has become the Advocate before God.
God has to forgive us now. If He does not forgive, He will be
unrighteous. Today when I confess my sins, God is faithful
and righteous to forgive my sins. The Word of God tells me
that the Lord Jesus has died. God has to be faithful to His
own Word. He also has to be righteous regarding the work

of the Lord Jesus. That is why He has to forgive our sins and cleanse us from all unrighteousness.

God's forgiveness of our sins is based entirely upon the blood of the Lord Jesus. The sins of the sinners are forgiven through the blood of the Lord Jesus. The sins of the Christians are likewise forgiven through the blood of the Lord Jesus. Because the Lord Jesus is the Savior, God can forgive the sins of the sinners. Because the Lord is the Advocate, God can forgive the sins of the believers. In the Lord Jesus' being both the Advocate and the Savior, it is His blood that grants us forgiveness of sins and justification.

CONFESSION

What then is confession? The apostle did not say that confession is praying that God would forgive our sins. Many prayers and pleadings before God for forgiveness are not confessions. Nor did the apostle say that confession is just to utter something with our mouth. What the apostle said was that we have to acknowledge the sin, to treat the sin as sin. Confession means that we stand on the same ground as God does, admitting before God that our deed is indeed a sin. The moment you confess your sin, you will be forgiven. To confess is not to plead for forgiveness. Forgiveness is the Lord Jesus' business. What you have to do is judge the sin as sin. You have to judge it, acknowledge it, and confess that it is wrong. You have to take sin as sin and treat sin as sin. What you must confess before God is that a sin is indeed a sin. If you confess your sins, God is faithful and righteous to forgive all your sins and unrighteousness. Just as a sinner receives the forgiveness of sins through the work of the Lord Jesus, a Christian receives the forgiveness of sins from God by judging his sin as sin and through the work of Christ upon him. Simply put, confession is our saying that something is sin because God says that it is sin. For example, suppose a brother's child goes out into the street and plays with some bad children. Because he picks up foul language and gets into mischief, the brother brings in the children who have been leading his son to do these things and tells them that they are wrong and that they should no longer play with his child.

He also tells his son not to play with them anymore. The child says that he wishes to confess that he is wrong and asks for forgiveness. But although he says this with his mouth, in his heart he is thinking of a way to sneak out the back door to go out and play again. He does not stand one with his father. At issue here is not forgiveness, but whether or not we acknowledge something as sin.

Confession means that whatever God considers as sin I also consider as sin. It means that I say the same as what God has said. If God says that it is wrong, I say that it is wrong also. Confession is your recognition and declaration of sin. When you do it, God forgives your sins and cleanses you from all unrighteousness. He is not forgiving you because of your confession; He is forgiving you because of the work of the Lord Jesus. His blood is the basis of everything in this matter. But through confession, the blood produces forgiveness. Salvation is by the blood through faith. But forgiveness is by the blood through confession. This is like saying that tap water comes by the source of the water department through the pipes. In the same way, forgiveness comes by the blood through confession.

THE OLD TESTAMENT TYPE OF THE RED HEIFER

There is a kind of cleansing in the Old Testament which is a type of the forgiveness of believers in the New Testament. The words in 1 John 1 and 2 are typified in the Old Testament. Let us read what can be considered as the only portion in the Old Testament dealing with the forgiveness of the Christians' sins.

Numbers 19:1-13 says, "And Jehovah spoke to Moses and to Aaron, saying, This is the statute of the law which Jehovah has commanded, saying, Tell the sons of Israel to bring you a red heifer without blemish, in which there is no defect, and upon which a yoke has never come. And you shall give her to Eleazar the priest, and she shall be taken outside the camp and slaughtered before him; and Eleazar the priest shall take some of her blood with his finger, and shall sprinkle some of her blood toward the front of the tent of meeting seven times. And the heifer shall be burned in his sight; her skin, her flesh, and her blood, with her dung, shall be burned; and the priest shall take cedar wood and hyssop and scarlet, and cast them into the midst of the burning of the heifer. Then the priest shall wash his clothes and bathe his flesh in water, and afterwards he shall come into the camp; and the priest shall be unclean until evening. And he who burns it shall wash his clothes in water and bathe his flesh in water, and shall be unclean until evening. And a man who is clean shall gather up the ashes of the heifer, and place them outside the camp in a clean place; and they shall be kept for the assembly of the sons of Israel for the water for impurity; it is a purification of sin. And he who gathers the ashes of the heifer shall wash his clothes, and be unclean until evening. And this shall be to the sons of Israel, and to the stranger who sojourns among them, for a perpetual statute. He who touches the dead body of any man shall be unclean seven days; he shall purify himself with the water on the third day and on the seventh day, and so be clean; but if he does not purify himself on the third day and on the seventh day, he will not be clean. Whoever touches a dead person, the body of any man who has died, and does not purify himself, defiles the tabernacle of Jehovah, and that person shall be cut off from Israel; because the water for impurity was not sprinkled upon him, he shall be unclean; his uncleanness is still on him."

In Numbers 19 a sacrifice is described. This sacrifice is the most unique sacrifice in the Old Testament. The book of Numbers is not a book on offerings. The book on offerings is Leviticus. But this sacrifice is not mentioned in Leviticus. Rather, it is mentioned in Numbers. We know that the Passover lamb was slain in Egypt. This typifies the Lord Jesus' death for our sins. At Mount Sinai God showed us again what the Passover lamb is. The five offerings in Leviticus are the Passover lamb analyzed and broken down. They show us the different aspects of the Lord Jesus and how He satisfies God's requirements in redeeming man's sins. All of these are for the sinners and were spoken of at Mount Sinai. The book of Numbers, however, is a book on the wilderness. It is a history of the children of Israel's wandering in the wilderness of Paran. There the children of Israel lived as sojourners in the wilderness. They were a nation sojourning in the world. There God gave them another sacrifice, which is the sacrifice of the red heifer.

All offerings are for God, and thus their blood is to be poured out. This is the only sacrifice whose blood is first sprinkled directly before the tabernacle and then burnt up. Most offerings are of male bulls and goats. But this sacrifice alone is a heifer, a female cow. Most sacrifices have no color specification. But this sacrifice has to be of a specific color; it must be a red heifer. Most sacrifices are offered on the altar. Only this sacrifice is burned outside the camp. Other sacrifices are for the forgiveness of sins. But the second half of this sacrifice is for cleansing. The five offerings of Leviticus describe the Passover lamb. They are prepared for sinners. This is why they are recorded in Exodus and Leviticus. This sacrifice, however, is prepared for the people of God. This is why it is recorded in Numbers. It is a sacrifice for the experience of God's people in the way of the wilderness. The other sacrifices are for sin. Only this sacrifice is for the filth in the wilderness. Other sacrifices are male animals. This sacrifice is female. Everything that is related to sinners is male, and everything that is related to God's people is female (Deut. 21:3-9). Leviticus 5:6 says that a female goat can be offered up as a trespass offering. The trespass offering is not just for sinners, but is frequently for believers. It is not like the sin offering, which is strictly for sinners. The trespass offering is for both sinners and believers. When something is offered up for God's people, it can be female. This is the regulation in the Old Testament.

This sacrifice, though dealing with man's offenses toward God, is actually offered up for believers. The color red signifies redemption before God. This sacrifice is not offered on the altar, because it is not for sinners. A sinner has to pass through the altar before he can come to God. This sacrifice is burned outside the camp. The camp is the place where the people of God are. Hence, the camp is a type of the church. To be outside the camp is to be cut off from the fellowship. But if you are cut off from the fellowship, a sacrifice is waiting for you. This is a sacrifice to deal with the believers' sins. It is for the restoration of fellowship.

Let us now consider the sacrifice itself. This sacrifice is of two parts. In the first part, the blood of the sacrifice is offered. In the second part, the sacrifice is burned. The first part begins from the second half of Numbers 19:2. "Tell the sons of Israel to bring you a red heifer without blemish, in which there is no defect, and upon which a yoke has never come." All those who understand the Bible know that this refers to the Lord Jesus. Hebrews 10 indicates that this red heifer refers to the Lord Jesus. What are the Lord Jesus' qualifications to become this sacrifice? Numbers 19:2 says that this sacrifice was to be without spot and without blemish and was never to have come under a yoke. Being without spot and blemish refers to His life. Never having come under a yoke refers to His work. In life He is without blemishes. In work He has never been under a yoke. In His life and person, the Lord Jesus is without spot and blemish. Not only is He without blemish, but also in His experience He is clean, that is, He has never been under a yoke. He is a clean man, and He has a clean experience. Many people are without blemish, but they have been yoked. But in His experience, the Lord Jesus was never yoked. He never touched the things of sin. He was never oppressed by sin or dominated by sin. He was never provoked to sin. He is completely free. Tonight we cannot say this for ourselves, for we are not free people. We have been oppressed by sin and have been dominated by sin. We have been provoked by sin and are not our own masters. The Lord Jesus has no spots. Only the Lord Jesus has never been put under the yoke of sin.

This is a heifer, a female cow, signifying that this sacrifice was offered up for believers. It is red. That means it is offered up for the redemption of sin. In the Bible, red signifies the redemption of sin. Every time the Bible mentions scarlet or red, it implies sin. The woman in Revelation 18 rides on a scarlet beast and wears a scarlet robe. These refer to her sins.

Numbers 19:4 tells us what happens after the heifer is slaughtered. "And Eleazar the priest shall take some of her

blood with his finger, and shall sprinkle some of her blood
toward the front of the tent of meeting seven times." The
priest did not do many things. He only sprinkled some blood
before God in the tabernacle. This shows us that the death
of the Lord Jesus has satisfied the requirements of God. The
blood was not sprinkled on the children of Israel. It was
sprinkled directly before the tent of meeting. The tabernacle
is the place where God met with the Israelites. It is a type
of the fellowship between God and man. Where God's
tabernacle is, there God is also. Christ is the tabernacle; He
is God living among men. He is full of God's grace and truth.
He tabernacled among us (John 1:14). This is the fellowship.
How can we have fellowship? There must be the blood, that
is, sin must be judged. If there is no blood, man cannot come
to God.

There are only two ways for man to come to God. Either
he comes without sin, or he comes with the blood. If you are
without sin, you can come to God in bold strides, and He can
do nothing to you. But if you have sin, there must be the
shedding of the blood (Heb. 9:22), because God must judge
sin. If sin is not judged, man cannot have fellowship with
God. God cannot overlook man's sins. God cannot let man's
sins go by. If man has sin, he must come to God with the
blood. God is a judging God. Without passing through
judgment, sin cannot be removed. Judgment demands the
blood. Therefore, there must be the shedding of the blood
before fellowship can be recovered. The blood was sprinkled
seven times. Seven signifies perfection. The death of the Lord
Jesus has satisfied God; His blood is sufficient to wash away
our sins. Here all the problems are completely solved. God's
righteous requirements are met. God said that the work is
done. This is the work of the Lord Jesus on the cross. It has
been done once and is forever finished. There is no need for
another red heifer to die. It is good enough for one red heifer
to die. In the first part of this offering we see that the
sprinkling of the blood signifies that the problem of the sinner
is solved. This part of the offering is the same as all the
other offerings in the Old Testament. They are all just the
Passover lamb.

Now we have to consider the second part of the offering, which shows us what is to be done for the sins of the believers. Numbers 19:5 says, "And the heifer shall be burned in his sight." This is most unique, for the heifer was not simply burned, but "her skin, her flesh, and her blood, with her dung, shall be burned; and the priest shall take cedar wood and hyssop and scarlet, and cast them into the midst of the burning of the heifer." God judged sin. After a little of the blood was sprinkled, the rest of the blood was poured into the fire. Then the whole heifer was also cast into the fire. The priest burned the whole heifer—skin, flesh, blood, dung, and all. In addition, cedar wood, hyssop, and scarlet were all cast into the midst of the burning. In verse 9 we are told what happened after the heifer was burned: "A man who is clean shall gather up the ashes of the heifer, and place them outside the camp in a clean place; and they shall be kept for the assembly of the sons of Israel for the water for impurity; it is a purification of sin." After the heifer was slaughtered, the blood was applied. But after the heifer was burned and became ashes, the ashes were to be applied.

What are ashes? Ashes are the final state of everything in the world. I am not referring to the facts of chemistry, but to our everyday experience. Ashes are the last state of all things. If a table undergoes corruption again and again, its last state will be ashes. Hence, ashes represent the final state. When something has reached its very end, and cannot be changed to something else anymore, it is ashes.

Everything of the heifer is burned. Note particularly the blood. In these ashes are the skin, the flesh, and the blood. This means that in these ashes are the redemption of Christ and the eternal efficacy of His redemption. Christ is eternally efficacious before God. He has become the ashes. The shedding of His blood is eternally efficacious. Even the blood has become ashes. The work of redemption is finished. The red heifer portrays the Lord's redemptive work, and this work has now become ashes.

There are three other things added to the offering: the cedar wood, the hyssop, and the scarlet. In the Bible, when cedar wood and hyssop are put together, it denotes the whole created universe. First Kings 4:33 says that Solomon had great wisdom. He spoke of all the trees, from the cedar tree to the hyssop. He went from alpha to omega. He exhausted the whole subject. The Bible uses the cedar tree and the hyssop to represent the whole world. Putting the cedar wood and the hyssop into the fire means that when the Lord Jesus was judged for sin, not only was He burned, but all of us were burned as well. God has judged all men in the person of Jesus of Nazareth. When the fire passed over Him, you and I, the cedar wood and the hyssop, all, passed through the same fire. Everything in the world, whether great or small, sweet or bitter, rich or poor, was laid on Him and judged by God. Here scarlet was also put in the fire. Isaiah 1:18 says that our sins are as scarlet. Hence, scarlet denotes sin. Not only has God judged us, but He has judged our sins as well. All sins were included with the Lord Jesus. When He was judged by God, our sins were judged as well. All the problems related to sin were also judged. Hence, the casting of the cedar wood, the hyssop, and the scarlet into the fire indicates that the whole world and all the sins of the world have passed through the fire with the Lord Jesus and have become ashes. The ashes include all the work of the Lord Jesus. They also include us and our sins. These ashes are eternally efficacious. Hence, this work has an efficaciousness that meets all of God's demands before Him. These ashes were kept outside the camp in a clean place.

From Numbers 19:11 on we are told about the function of the ashes. "He who touches the dead body of any man shall be unclean seven days. He shall purify himself with the water on the third day..." Verse 9 tells us about this water for impurity. "And a man who is clean shall gather up the ashes of the heifer, and place them outside the camp in a clean place; and they shall be kept for the assembly of the sons of Israel for the water for impurity; it is a purification of sin." The impurity spoken of refers to the impurity of touching a dead body. Why is touching a dead body considered an impurity? It is because death is the evidence of sin. Without sin there would be no death. Therefore, where there is death, there is also sin. A dead body means that sin has done its work. The result of the work of sin is death. For this reason, the Old Testament uses leprosy as a symbol of curable sin and a dead body as a symbol of incurable sin. When a man is dead in sin and trespasses and therefore dead in his flesh, he is a dead body. The Lord Jesus talked about these dead ones. He said to let the dead bury the dead (Matt. 8:22). If you touch these dead ones, if you have intercourse with the world, if you build up a friendship with it, and if you have your living among it, you are touching dead bodies. If you touch dead bodies, you will surely be infected and defiled with impurities. When Christians sin and fail through touching the world, the ashes are needed.

The ashes are the work of the cross. They are put into the living water (Num. 19:17) and become the water for impurity. The living water typifies the Holy Spirit. Once while the children of Israel journeyed, they struck the rock and out came living water (Exo. 17:6). First Corinthians 10:4 says that the rock was Christ. Hence, the living water refers to what flows forth from Christ, which is the Holy Spirit. Taking the living water and making it the water for impurity means that there is the need for the power of the Holy Spirit to be upon us. Without the work of the Holy Spirit, the work of the Lord will be in vain. If there are only the ashes of the red heifer without the living water, they will not be of much use. With the work of the Lord Jesus, there is still the need of the Holy Spirit. Only by the mixing together of the two will we be purified and cleansed. The Lord Jesus does not have to die again. We merely apply the efficacy of the one-time work of the Lord for our cleansing. The ashes of the red heifer represent the eternal and immutable efficacy of the Lord's work on the cross. It is this efficacy that is cleansing us. Because the Lord Jesus has died, the efficacy of His ashes becomes eternal, and by the Holy Spirit He is now applying this efficacy to us.

Every time we sin, we do not have to bring a bull to God again. The efficacy of the Lord's work two thousand years ago continues until today. By those ashes we are cleansed.

What happens if a man is not cleansed? Numbers 19:12 says, "He shall purify himself with the water on the third day and on the seventh day, and so be clean; but if he does not purify himself the third day and on the seventh day, he will not be clean." Why is such a one not clean until the seventh day? The man cleanses himself on the third day, but he is not clean until the seventh day. He is not clean until the seventh day because the goal is the seventh day, not the third day. The third day is the day the Lord Jesus resurrected. After the Lord resurrected, He gave to us the word of the forgiveness of sin. What then is the seventh day? In the Bible the seventh day is the Sabbath. Hebrews 4:9 says that there is another Sabbath. This is the universal, great Sabbath, which will take place in the millennium. This means that a person who is not cleansed in the age of the Lord's resurrection will not be clean in the age of the kingdom. If he is cleansed today in the age of the Lord's resurrection, he will be clean on the seventh day, the age of the kingdom. The third day is for the seventh day. The problem is with the seventh day. The problem of eternity is settled. The problem of being God's children in this age is also settled. All other problems are settled. The only problem today is whether we will be clean in the kingdom.

At the end of this portion, Numbers 19:13 says, "Whoever touches a dead person, the body of any man who has died, and does not purify himself, defiles the tabernacle of Jehovah." What is the tabernacle of the Lord? The tabernacle of the Lord today is not a meeting hall or some chapel. The tabernacle of the Lord today is our body. If a man destroys his body, God will destroy him (1 Cor. 3:17). If a man defiles his body, God will say, "That person shall be cut off from Israel" (Num. 19:13b). Such a person will be rejected from Israel. It does not say he will be rejected from Egypt, but from Israel. This means that at the time the children of God reign in the kingdom, such a one will be kept outside. If a person is not clean today, he will be kept outside the kingdom in the future.

Following this we read: "Because the water for impurity was not sprinkled upon him, he shall be unclean; his uncleanness is still on him." All the unconfessed sins and all the sins that have not passed through the blood of the Lord

Jesus leave their uncleanness on the person. This uncleanness will cause one to lose his share in the coming kingdom. Conversely, those who have been cleansed by the water for impurity will be clean in the kingdom. Let me tell you one thing: No sin that has been repented of, that has been confessed and put under the blood of the Lord Jesus, and that has had the ashes applied to it, can ever raise its head at the judgment seat. The water for impurity is able to remove uncleanness because of the power of the blood in it. It is the power of redemption in this water that enables it to remove the uncleanness. Every sin that does not have the effectiveness of the Lord's redemption applied to it will leave uncleanness on the person until the "seventh day." Hence, do not let your sins remain on you. You must remove the uncleanness with the ashes of the Lord Jesus. I thank the Lord that the Son of God does not have to die for me anymore. By His ashes I am clean. But it is foolish as well as dangerous to allow any uncleanness to remain.

CHAPTER TWENTY-SIX

HOW GOD DEALS
WITH THE BELIEVERS' SINS—
FOOT-WASHING

THE ASHES OF THE RED HEIFER
IN THE OLD TESTAMENT

In Numbers 19 God shows us that if a man touches a dead body, he is defiled and must cleanse himself with the ashes of the red heifer. The way to apply the ashes is to put them in the running water (Num. 19:17). If a man has any impurity, the water with the ashes can be sprinkled on him, and the man will be cleansed. The work of Christ is completed. There is no need for Christ to be crucified again. Our need now is to apply the ashes to us, that is, to apply the efficacy of this work to us. The way to apply it is to mix it with the Holy Spirit. Only the work of the Holy Spirit can transfer its effectiveness over to us.

Hence, at issue today is not the work of the Lord Jesus. At issue today is the work of the Holy Spirit. There is no question about the Lord's dying for us. The question is whether or not this work has produced an effect on us, whether or not the Holy Spirit has applied the work of the Lord Jesus to us. When we confess our sins, the Holy Spirit applies the Lord's work of redemption to us. He will cause us to think of the Lord and to realize how complete His work is. The Holy Spirit reminds us in our heart of the redemptive work of the Lord. He causes us to remember and to enter into this truth. By this our heart will have peace and joy. The Holy Spirit comes and applies the work of the ashes, that is, the eternal work of the Lord Jesus, to us. The Lord has accomplished all the work. There is no need to ask for anything or to do anything. Now when we confess our sins, the Holy Spirit comes and causes us to consider this truth so that we can receive the benefits of the Lord's redemption.

FOOT-WASHING IN THE NEW TESTAMENT

Not only does the Old Testament show us the cleansing by the death of the Lord Jesus, but in the New Testament the Lord Jesus also did something to show us the same thing. John 13 shows us a picture of what a Christian should do when he sins. John 13:1 says, "Now before the Feast of the Passover, Jesus, knowing that His hour had come for Him to depart out of this world unto the Father, having loved His own who were in the world, He loved them to the uttermost." After this word, the Lord Jesus did something which shows not only His love, but His love to the uttermost. John 13 is different from John 3. John 3 is about God's initial love. John 13 is about God's uttermost love. Once God loves His children, He loves them to the uttermost.

John 13:3-10 says, "Jesus, knowing that the Father had given all into His hands and that He had come forth from God and was going to God, rose from supper and laid aside His outer garments; and taking a towel, He girded Himself; then He poured water into the basin and began to wash the disciples' feet and to wipe them with the towel with which He was girded. He came then to Simon Peter. Peter said to Him, Lord, do You wash my feet? Jesus answered and said to him, What I am doing you do not know now, but you will know after these things. Peter said to Him, You shall by no means wash my feet forever. Jesus answered him, Unless I wash you, you have no part with Me. Simon Peter said to Him, Lord, not my feet only, but also my hands and my head. Jesus said to him, He who is bathed has no need except to wash his feet, but is wholly clean."

Foot-washing has two meanings in the Bible. Jesus' washing of the disciples' feet has one meaning, and the disciples' washing of each other's feet has another meaning. To wash each other's feet is to recover one another and to revive one another. Jesus' washing the disciples' feet has another meaning.

All of us have shoes and socks; therefore, foot-washing is not that necessary for us. But some of us come from the southeast Asian countries. There foot-washing is necessary because many wear sandals only. They do not wear socks. The Jews were like the southeastern Asians; they wore sandals and did not have socks. Often they walked through desert lands, and their feet were constantly dirty. Not only did their feet get dirty when they traveled, but sometimes their feet got dirty when they walked across the hall immediately after a bath. Even when their body was already clean, their feet still needed washing before they would be wholly clean.

What does the Lord Jesus want to show us in this picture? Verse 10 says, "Jesus said to him, He who is bathed has no need except to wash his feet, but is wholly clean." Who are those who are bathed? Ananias told Paul to rise up and be baptized for the washing away of his sins (Acts 22:16). Bathing in the Bible signifies the full cleansing from sin of a person when he believes in the Lord Jesus. Last night we saw the slaughtering and the burning of the heifer. The slaughtering is for our redemption, and the burning is for our cleansing. Tonight we also have to consider two kinds of cleansing. One is foot-washing. The other is bathing. There are two sides to the Lord's work—the slaughtering and the burning; and when we apply the effects of this work to us, there are also two sides—the foot-washing and the bathing. He cleansed us with His own blood. This work of redemption was accomplished once for all. When we believe in and receive Him, we are washed in the pool of His blood and are fully cleansed. Thank the Lord that we have all taken the bath. All our sins have been washed away by the Lord Jesus. But now that we have believed in the Lord and have been washed, while we are on our journey in the wilderness, we cannot avoid coming in contact with the world. We cannot avoid picking up impurities. In our journeying in the wilderness, spontaneously we come into contact with the world, and spontaneously the dust of the earth defiles our feet.

BATHING AND FOOT-WASHING

Although we Christians are bathed once only, the Bible

shows us that foot-washing happens many times. There is
only one bathing, but there are many foot-washings. It is like
the cleansing: There is only one cleansing by the blood, but
there are many cleansings by the water of the ashes. The
accomplished redemption of Christ occurred once only. But
there are many applications by the Holy Spirit of this
accomplished work to us. We are bathed only once, and all
our sins are washed. But it takes many foot-washings to wash
away all the dirt that we pick up on the wilderness journey.
There needs to be only one bathing. But foot-washing is a
daily work before the Lord. Foot-washing is a washing that
comes about by the Word of God, through the work of the
Holy Spirit, and based upon the work of the Lord Jesus. If
we have been cleansed once by His blood, we must continue
to be washed daily by His blood as well. The Lord Jesus does
not have to come and do another work. We are cleansed again
and again based on that one work. It is not the ashes that
are cleansing us but the water of the ashes. The ashes of
the red heifer are the mark of our judgment.

God did not substitute our judgment with the judgment
of the Lord Jesus. Rather, He judged us in Christ Jesus.
Today man thinks that the Lord Jesus died in place of man;
but actually, we died in and with the Lord Jesus. In other
words, we are judged in Christ. This alone will cleanse us.
My daily cleansing is based on the death of the Lord Jesus.

We know that we have taken a bath, that is, our sins have
been cleansed. Once we are saved, we are eternally saved.
All the problems are solved. What then should we do when
we touch the dirt while living on earth and coming into contact
with the world every day? We all cannot be like the thief on
the cross, who went straight to Paradise without his feet ever
touching the earth after he was cleansed by the blood. Most
people are not saved while on their deathbeds. Most still have
to take the wilderness journey. Every one of us knows that
while we take the wilderness journey, we should not sin. But
sinning is a fact with all of us. As a result, our feet get dirty.
Many times we are rash and speak words that we should not
speak. Many times we have improper thoughts. Thus, we
admit that we are defiled. But God has prepared the

foot-washing of the Lord Jesus for us. This is not just a sign of His love for us, but a sign of His love to the uttermost. He loved us; hence, He was crucified for us. Now He loves us to the uttermost; hence, He washes our feet. Figuratively speaking, foot-washing is not the love before marriage. Foot-washing is the love after marriage. He causes us to be continually clean before Him. This is why the Lord said that he who has been bathed will be wholly clean once his feet are washed. We thank the Lord that His Son has given us a bath already.

The Lord allowed Peter's foolishness to be manifested as a lesson for us. When He came to Peter, Peter said, "Are You going to wash my feet?" Peter thought that this was a matter of politeness and courtesy. The Lord said that Peter would not understand what He did then but would understand later. There is much spiritual truth here. When the Holy Spirit comes, we will see. Now we are bewildered. All we see is a basin of water and the Lord's washing. We do not see what they mean. In the future, however, we will understand. But Peter always had his opinions. He exclaimed that the Lord would never wash his feet. The Lord told him that the foot-washing was very important. If the Lord did not wash Peter's feet that night, Peter would have no part with Him.

Do not think that it is enough to have a bath once and be cleansed by the blood of the Lord once. Do not think that we can get by loosely when we are defiled by the dirt on our way through the world. The Lord said that if our feet are not washed, we will have no part with Him. This means His fellowship with us today will be terminated. His fellowship with us in the future kingdom will also be lost. How important are the daily cleansings. We must allow the Lord to wash our feet every day. We have to come back every day to be recovered and to get the application of the power of Christ's redemption. We do not need the blood of the Lord Jesus to wash us again before God. The Lord's work before God has been finished once and for all. But we can experience the washing many times. The blood of His Son washes our sins again and again continuously. Therefore, we must have our feet washed every day. We have to take care of the cleanliness of our feet every day.

Peter was like we are. He always went to extremes. He went to one end at one time and then to the other end at another time. At one moment he said that the Lord would never wash his feet. Then when he heard the Lord say that he would have no part with Him if there were no foot-washing, he asked that his head and his hands be washed as well. The Lord Jesus showed him that this other extreme is wrong also. The Lord said that he who is bathed has no need except to wash his feet. No one can repent and believe in the Lord twice. No one can be regenerated twice. No one can receive the Savior twice. Once you come to the Lord Jesus and accept Him as Savior, that is enough. Perhaps you doubt for a few days. Perhaps you think that when you accepted Him as Savior the last time, you did not do a good enough job, and perhaps you begin to doubt after a few days; you want to accept Him again. But the Lord said that there is no need. The head does not need to be washed again, and the hands do not need to be washed again. The Lord Jesus said that those who have taken a bath only need to have their feet washed in order to be wholly clean. We only need one bath for the whole body. Although we touch the world and dirty our feet often, this does not affect the cleanliness of our whole body. There needs to be only one bath for the whole body. The bath cannot be repeated. Hallelujah! Even if you walk in the mud and your feet become black, it will not affect the cleanliness of your whole body. Your body does not need to be cleansed again. Once you have received the Lord Jesus as the Savior, your body is cleansed. From then on, you do not need to wash your body again. When a man is cleansed once, he is cleansed forever. No one can deny this. One's feet can get dirty, and he can be cut off from the fellowship of the Lord. He can have no share in the kingdom, but the whole body is still clean. All those who are bathed need to wash only their feet, and they will be fully clean. What we are doing day by day is looking back at our Savior. The Lord Jesus has done an eternal work. Day by day as we live on earth, we need to keep only our feet clean and free from dirt.

If we pick up some dirt by accident, we can still receive a daily washing, so that we can enjoy uninterrupted fellowship with the Lord and reign with Him tomorrow. This is our way. May the Lord keep our feet clean day after day, so that we can glorify His name here on earth.